ROUND ABOUT JAMESTOWN

Historical Sketches of the Lower Virginia Peninsula

J. E. Davis

HERITAGE BOOKS
2007

HERITAGE BOOKS
AN IMPRINT OF HERITAGE BOOKS, INC.

Books, CDs, and more—Worldwide

For our listing of thousands of titles see our website
at
www.HeritageBooks.com

A Facsimile Reprint
Published 2007 by
HERITAGE BOOKS, INC.
Publishing Division
65 East Main Street
Westminster, Maryland 21157-5026

Copyright © 1907 J. E. Davis

— Publisher's Notice —
In reprints such as this, it is often not possible to remove blemishes from the original. We feel the contents of this book warrant its reissue despite these blemishes and hope you will agree and read it with pleasure.

International Standard Book Number: 978-0-7884-2219-5

PREFACE

IT is perhaps essential that the term "Lower Virginia Peninsula" as used in this book should be defined. I mean by it that part of Virginia lying between the James and the York Rivers and extending from Jamestown and Williamsburg to Fortress Monroe, which is the portion occupied by the first English settlers in America and of special interest on that account. It is for this reason that but few facts in the history of Norfolk and Richmond are mentioned, and those chiefly the ones which have some connection with the section chosen for more detailed description.

In placing before the public these chapters of early Virginia history I wish to express my indebtedness to the friends who have urged their publication, and especially to those who have verified the facts contained in them. Prominent among the latter are Rev. C. B. Bryan, D.D., of Petersburg, formerly rector of St. John's Church, Hampton; Dr. Lyon G. Tyler, of William and Mary College; Major I. N. Lewis, of the Artillery School at Fort Monroe; Miss Lottie Garrett, of Williamsburg; Mrs. Janie Hope Marr, of Lexington; and Miss Cary, of Richmond.

The principal authorities consulted were Captain John Smith, Stith, Bruce, Howe, Fiske, John Esten Cook, and Rhodes. For the use of Strachey's History of Travaile into Virginia, Hening's Statutes, and other rare books, as well as old magazines and newspapers in the excellent Virginia collection in the Library of William and Mary College, I am indebted to the courtesy of President Tyler.

Most of the half-tones used in illustration are loaned by the *Southern Workman*, of Hampton, Virginia, in which magazine these sketches first appeared.

J. E. DAVIS.

Hampton, Va., May 1, 1907.

CONTENTS.

CHAPTER		PAGE
I	JAMESTOWN, PAST AND PRESENT	7
II	HAMPTON ROADS AND THE JAMESTOWN TERCENTENNIAL	16
III	OLD POINT COMFORT AND FORTRESS MONROE	23
IV	OLD KECOUGHTAN	30
V	THE VIRGINIA PENINSULA IN THE SEVENTEENTH CENTURY	38
VI	PIRATES OF THE VIRGINIA CAPES	45
VII	THE VIRGINIA PENINSULA IN THE EIGHTEENTH CENTURY	51
VIII	THE VIKINGS OF VIRGINIA	58
IX	HAMPTON IN THREE WARS	67
X	HAMPTON SCHOOLS BETWEEN 1850 AND 1870	73
XI	VIRGINIA'S SECOND COLONIAL CAPITAL	80
XII	YORKTOWN, THE WATERLOO OF THE REVOLUTION	91
XIII	RICHMOND AND THE JAMES RIVER PLANTATIONS	98

ILLUSTRATIONS.

	PAGE
THE JAMESTOWN TOWER	10
THE GRAVEYARD AT JAMESTOWN	14
RIP RAPS, OR FORT WOOL	20
FORT MONROE, SHOWING THE OLD WATER BATTERY	24
THE HYGEIA HOTEL	28
AT THE MOUTH OF JAMES RIVER	32
SHIRLEY ON THE JAMES	36
THE OLDEST ENGLISH COMMUNION SERVICE IN AMERICA	38
THE OLDEST CUSTOM HOUSE IN AMERICA (YORKTOWN)	42
THE HISTORIC NELSON MANSION, YORKTOWN	44
CARTER'S GROVE, JAMES RIVER	52
AN EIGHTEENTH CENTURY MANOR HOUSE	54
ST. JOHN'S CHURCH, HAMPTON	56
ST. PAUL'S CHURCH, NORFOLK	60
ST. JOHN'S AT THE CLOSE OF THE CIVIL WAR	68
HAMPTON HOSPITAL	70
CHESAPEAKE FEMALE COLLEGE	74
THE BUTLER SCHOOL FOR CONTRABANDS	76
THE BEGINNINGS OF HAMPTON INSTITUTE	78
WILLIAM AND MARY COLLEGE	82
BRUTON PARISH CHURCH	84
THE COURTHOUSE AT WILLIAMSBURG	88
THE MAIN STREET OF YORKTOWN	92
THE MOORE HOUSE, YORKTOWN	96
THE OLD CAPITOL, RICHMOND	98
HISTORIC ST. JOHN'S, RICHMOND	100
LOWER BRANDON	102

I
JAMESTOWN, PAST AND PRESENT

WHAT pictures are conjured up by the name Jamestown, what recollections crowd upon us, what contrasts come unbidden to the mind! Three hundred years ago in this "Cradle of the Republic" lay an infant country, tiny and weak, without money, without food, with nothing, indeed, but an immense though hidden vitality and an unbounded persistence which gave it power to grow in spite of adverse circumstances, in spite of every imaginable drawback, into a mighty nation, a world-power, stretching out its beneficent hands into the remotest corners of the earth. In imagination we sail down the Thames in December 1606, with that little handful of English settlers. First southward to the Azores and then westward we travel for many months, until finally Captain Newport pilots us through the Virginia capes, and the long, hard voyage is ended on April 26, 1607, when we disembark on a sandy spit of land and name the spot Cape Henry. Here we rest while the sealed orders of the London Company are opened and we learn that we are to settle much further inland. We board the vessel again and sail across the Bay to the broad river which we name the James, and whose shores we explore for many a mile seeking dutifully for a suitable place for a settlement. This we think we find at an attractive spot about thirty miles from the mouth of the river, where the water is deep so close to the shore that we can tie our ships to the trees, and here we disembark on a beautiful May day. A Virginia spring is full of promise, and all is so fair on this charming morning that we do not think to remind our friends that we are disobeying the order which says that we shall not settle in a low or moist place, and we busy ourselves in giving thanks to God in our improvised church under the sailcloth, for our safe arrival.

Now there are trees to be felled and a fort to be built, for yonder, across the narrow neck of land, we often catch glimpses of savages, and though they come among us on friendly errands, we cannot trust them. And so, in a month's time, we build our fort and inside place our houses in straight rows. We are content with very plain houses; indeed they are not much more than huts, but we roof them with marsh grass and pile earth on top to keep them dry. Finally we build us a chapel in the middle of the enclosure, and though it is but a homely thing like a barn and we roof it, as we do our own houses, with grass and earth, in it we can worship God and praise Him for preserving us thus far. But alas! there are dissensions among our leaders; the malaria of the swamps that we forgot to consider attacks many of our number; we have not enough to eat; and we must stop our building and clearing of land to lay one and another in his grave. Before the end of the summer we bury over sixty of our companions and those of us who are left wonder how soon we shall follow.

Jamestown, Past and Present

We live on as we can, having much to do and little strength with which to do it, seeing more English come to join us with many mouths to feed and little enough to put in them. Our leaders fight among themselves and we have no one in command whom we can respect. We have fire after fire which destroys our property and we grow discouraged trying to replace it. In the cold of winter many die from exposure and we pull down even our palisades to use for firewood. Our supplies give out entirely and the people live on roots and herbs until things finally come to such a pass that even dead human bodies are eaten by the most desperate. Of the five hundred people who have come to the Colony but sixty are left, scarcely able to totter about the place. We decide to abandon the settlement and we start back to England, glad to flee from our misery. But before we reach the capes we meet Lord de la Warre, who has come to be our governor. He has plenty of provisions and he takes us back to our ruined settlement to make a fresh start.

New fortifications were now built by the colonists and the houses were repaired. Cedar pews and a walnut altar were placed in the church and every Sunday it was decorated with flowers. A bell was hung in the tower, which not only called the people to church, but notified them when to begin and stop work. Instead of the system of communism which had prevailed the colonists were given land of their own and were obliged to cultivate it. Industry and thrift began to prevail and a repetition of the famine became well-nigh impossible. New settlers arrived and the Colony began to expand. By 1619 two thousand persons were

Jamestown, Past and Present

living in Virginia and they called for self-government, being tired of the tyranny of royal governors. Governor Yeardley issued writs for the election of a General Assembly and the first legislative body in America met in the Jamestown church in July of that year. Just after this meeting, in curious juxtaposition, came the first cargo of Negro slaves; and it was in this year also that there arrived from England a shipload of English maidens as wives for the colonists. Each young woman was free to exercise her choice, but no suitor who met with approval could take his bride unless able to pay the cost of her voyage—one hundred and twenty pounds of tobacco. Thus one year saw in the infant colony the establishment of the home, of a free representative government, and of the institution of slavery.

With the beginning of the culture of tobacco and the expansion of the Colony, Jamestown came to be chiefly a place for the assembling of the legislature and for holding court. A courthouse was built and in this the House of Burgesses met. At such times the little village almost earned its title of town, but the permanent population after 1623 was only about one hundred persons, who lived in brick houses of fair size and style. The first brick church, whose ruined tower is to-day the chief relic of old Jamestown, was built in 1639. It was a very plain and unpretentious chapel, rectangular in shape with a high-pitched roof. The aisles were paved with brick and the chancel with tiles. All attempts to increase the size of the town failed and after being destroyed three times by fire, the second time during Bacon's Rebellion in 1676, it was never

THE JAMESTOWN TOWER

rebuilt. The climate remained unhealthy and the conviction gradually grew that it would be wise to remove the capital to a more salubrious situation. This was found in Middle Plantation, now Williamsburg, which was made the capital of Virginia in 1698. By 1700 the removal was complete, so that for over two hundred years there has been no town on Jamestown Island.

Since the island was abandoned the river has done its best to obliterate all traces of the "Cradle of the Republic." Its work has at last, however, been interfered with, and patriotic women, under the name of the Association for the Preservation of Virginia Antiquities, have taken steps to rescue from oblivion this "first American metropolis." It was not until 1900, however, after fifty or sixty acres of the island, including the sites of the first landing place and the first and second forts, together with a part of the earliest settlement, had been worn away by the unrestrained action of the water, that this society succeeded in inducing the Government to build a sea wall to prevent further encroachments by the river. This was begun in 1901 and finished in 1905. Outside of this breakwater, two hundred and ninety feet from the shore, stands a lone cypress tree which in 1846 stood on the shore above high water mark.

One who wishes to make a pilgrimage to Jamestown now may follow in the wake of Captain Newport's little vessels, across Hampton Roads, full of historic memories, not only of Colonial times but also of events connected with the great wars of our history; past Newport News at the mouth of the James; and up the river which, could it speak, would have many a pathetic or romantic tale to tell. The names of the places on either bank bring back crowding memories of events of early Colonial days. On Lower Chippoke's Creek on the south side stands "Bacon's Castle," which, though not visible from the river, is one of the most interesting houses in Virginia. It was fortified by Bacon's friends during his rebellion. Further on are Basse's Choice, Pace's Pains, Archer's Hope, Martin's Hundred, and many other places that perpetuate the names of early settlers and which were represented in the General Assembly. Jamestown had reason to be grateful to the owner of the plantation of Pace's Pains, for it was he who saved the capital in the massacre of 1622, a converted Indian of his household having revealed the plot against the settlers.

On landing at Jamestown Island we give ourselves up to the task of rebuilding and repeopling the little town which speaks so eloquently to every American citizen. Turning to the left, for there the tower beckons, we enter the church enclosure. Here are the foundation walls of three of the five Jamestown churches and we examine with reverent interest the inner line of bricks, which we are told supported the wooden walls of the third Colonial church, the one in which met the first General Assembly of Virginia. We picture the governor, the deputy governor, the council, and the twenty-two Burgesses walking in dignified procession up the narrow aisle of the little church, as with stern, serious faces they proceed to transact their important business—a different scene indeed from the squalor and misery that filled the little village only

Jamestown, Past and Present

nine years before when Lord de la Warre saved the Colony. Was it here, we wonder, that Pocahontas was baptized and here that she was married? Alas! we learn that the little chapel which witnessed these scenes in the life of the Indian maiden who gave a touch of romance to the rude pioneer town, was inside the palisaded fort now buried under the restless waves of the James. It was just yonder, a stone's throw; while still further out in the water is hidden in the sand of the river bottom the spot on which the Jamestown settlers stepped from their ships. No Plymouth Rock this to withstand forever the action of the waves!

But let us turn again to the foundation walls and the pavements of the churches. Here are the tiles in the chancel of the wooden church and above them the two sets belonging to the two brick churches built on the same foundations. The tower was too massive to be destroyed when the town was fired in Bacon's Rebellion and still gives proof of its age in the "bonded" English brick of which it is made and in the loopholes near its top which indicate that it was used for defense from the Indians before Opechancanough removed that danger by his death. The worshipers who were wont to gather in these two churches now rest in the ancient graveyard outside. Here lie Dr. James Blair, "Commissary of Virginia and sometime minister of this parish," and his wife, Sarah, a daughter of Colonel Benjamin Harrison. A young sycamore starting between their tombstones carried with it, in the strength of its young life, a portion of Mrs. Blair's tombstone to the height of ten feet. This was accidentally released in 1895 and the tree has nearly closed the cavity, growing meanwhile to an enormous height and shading the whole graveyard. How typical of the gigantic growth of the infant republic born here! All about the old graveyard lie ancient stones, many of them in fragments, and some with their inscriptions quite indecipherable; beyond the enclosure, on the bank of the river, have been found human skeletons lying in such positions as to indicate that the graveyard once extended to the James. We are told that the present lot is about one-third the size of the original, and when we think of the thousands who perished at Jamestown in the early days we are not surprised that human remains have been found in nearly every part of the island.

Virginians have at length awakened to a realizing sense of the importance of preserving what remains of our first settlement. The ancient foundations of the town are being uncovered and every possible effort is being made to keep in good condition what is left of the sacred objects in the church enclosure. So far as possible the tombstones have been mended and the inscriptions made more legible, further vandalism being prevented by a caretaker who lives on the island.

Leaving the graveyard we walk thoughtfully past the earthworks of 1861, now grassgrown and forming part of a shady park peopled with mocking-birds and cardinals. Beyond, we come to the "third ridge" where recent excavations have laid bare the foundations of a row of houses, one of them being the State House in front of which Bacon drew up his soldiers and demanded his commission of Sir William Berkeley. The next one belonged to Colonel Philip Ludwell

The Graveyard at Jamestown

Jamestown, Past and Present

under whose direction the town was rebuilt after Bacon's Rebellion. As the excavations proceed it will be possible to picture the town as it looked during its last days.

No less than four monuments will be erected on Jamestown Island during the summer of 1907. Perhaps the most imposing will be the marble shaft erected by the Government to mark the scene of the nation's birth. Near it will be another shaft in memory of the first House of Burgesses, built by the Norfolk branch of the A. P. V. A. A bronze monument to Captain John Smith is to be erected on a terrace commanding a view of the river and near the monument to Pocahontas, the gift of the Pocahontas Memorial Association. Over the foundations of the brick churches the Colonial Dames of America have built a church as nearly as possible like the brick one erected in 1639. It contains many tablets, among them one to Rev. Robert Hunt, the first English minister in America. This church was presented to the A. P. V. A. on May 11, 1907. On May 13 the three hundredth anniversary of the landing at Jamestown was celebrated with appropriate ceremonies, Ambassador Bryce of England making the principal address.

II

HAMPTON ROADS AND THE JAMESTOWN TERCENTENNIAL

IT is more than three hundred years since the Susan Constant, the Godspeed, and the Discovery tied up to the trees overhanging the river at Jamestown. As we have seen, the settlement then made had but a short and precarious existence, lasting less than a century. The three hundredth anniversary of this English settlement, fraught with such portentous interest for these United States, is now (1907) being celebrated but not on the original site, for that is, as it ever was, a low marshy spot, unfit for habitation and offering no accommodations for visitors. Instead, the Jamestown Tercentennial is being held at Sewell's Point thirty miles down the river on the shore of Hampton Roads and nearer the place where the colonists first landed.

Captain John Smith tells us in his True Narration that venturing to land and explore the dense woods near the shore, he and his men were driven back by savages who came stealthily towards them creeping on all fours and carrying their bows in their mouths. Before they could regain the ship several of the company received severe arrow wounds, but they succeeded in so frightening the Indians with their powder and shot that they were not attacked again for some

Hampton Roads

time and were able later to penetrate several miles into the woods. On one occasion the Englishmen found some oysters roasting over a fire; they discovered also a "cannow" made out of a whole tree and measuring forty-five feet in length. Near the boat in the soft mud were quantities of mussels and oysters, and in a cleared place beyond they found strawberries "foure times bigger and better" than those they had known in England. Apparently satisfied that they had reached a land of plenty they set up a cross at the entrance to the bay, named the place Cape Henry, and continued for several days to explore the inlets and rivers on the south shore in a light shallop that they had built. On Cape Henry still stands the old lighthouse erected in 1691 on the very spot where the rude cross was set up in 1607 by the devout Englishmen in gratitude for the safe ending of their long journey. A tablet commemorating the landing has been placed on the lighthouse by the A. P. V. A.

The buildings of the Exposition at Sewell's Point are about twenty-five in number and are Colonial in architecture, with the Auditorium in the center capped by a low dome and flanked by the Historic and Historic Arts Buildings. The chief interest of the celebration lies in its historical features, although the naval display in Hampton Roads is doubtless the most striking. The grounds have much natural beauty and are enclosed by a unique fence covered with crimson rambler and honeysuckle. On the Exposition grounds is what is called Powhatan's Oak, known to be over three hundred years old, under which tradition says that the powerful Indian chief, who once ruled the

Hampton Roads

lower Virginia peninsula, sometimes held his councils of war. Also within the Fair grounds are the remains of the Confederate batteries which supported the Merrimac in its famous fight with the Monitor. With what tremendous interest would the men who manned the first American ironclads view the imposing array of the world's iron battleships now gathered on the very spot where, on March 9, 1862, the "Confederate ram" and the "Yankee cheese box" met in mortal combat and by that meeting revolutionized naval warfare!

Every schoolboy can describe the scene—can tell what happened the day before "On board of the Cumberland, sloop-of-war;" how the balls from the wooden ships and the shore batteries rebounded from the Merrimac's iron sides as if they were made of India rubber; how there was consternation in the Union fleet and alarm at the White House; how the Monitor reached Hampton Roads late on that terrible day; and how for four hours on the Sunday morning following, the hand-to-hand fight continued. "David," the people said, "had come out against Goliath." Captain John Wise who, standing on Sewell's Point, was an eye-witness of the fight says in the The End of an Era that the Monitor "presented the appearance of a saucy kingbird pecking at a very large and very black crow." Neither boat could ram the other and shells rebounded from the armor of both. Finally a shell from the Merrimac, passing between the iron logs of the pilot-house of the Monitor, blinded gallant Lieutenant Worden. The Monitor continued in action in spite of this disaster, and as she was able on account of her light draught to keep in shallow water where the Merrimac

Hampton Roads

could not follow, the latter soon retired to Norfolk. Both sides claimed the victory.

Standing at Sewell's Point one can look out over Hampton Roads, one of the most beautiful sheets of water in the world, and see that it is formed by three rivers—the James coming in from the west, the Nansemond from the south, and the Elizabeth from the east. To the north is Old Point Comfort protected by the guns of Fort Monroe, and midway between this and the Exposition grounds is the Rip Raps, or Fort Wool, an artificial island whose history is given in the following chapter. To the northwest may be seen the town of Hampton, the oldest continuous English settlement in America, and the water-fronts with some of the buildings of Hampton Institute and the National Soldiers' Home, while in the southwest at the mouth of the James rise the huge grain elevators of Newport News. This town, which now contains one of the largest dry docks in the world and is an important commercial center, was settled in 1621 by "Master Gookin out of Ireland who arrived with fifty men of his own and thirty passengers exceedingly well furnished with all sorts of provisions and cattle." He named it New Port Newce in honor of his friend, Sir William Newce of Ireland. A quaint old chronicler tells us that "at Nuportsnews the cotton trees in a yeere grow so thicke as one's arme and so high as a man; here anything that is planted doth prosper so well as in no place better."

Looking south from Sewell's Point one sees Craney Island at the mouth of the Elizabeth River. This was fortified during the War of 1812 to guard the city of

Hampton Roads

Norfolk, and the garrison was able to repulse an attack of the British under Admiral Cockburn in June 1813. Portions of an unfinished canal through which the British hoped to reach Norfolk without passing the harbor defenses may still be seen near Cape Henry. Craney Island, together with Sewell's and Lambeth's Points, was fortified by the Confederates during the Civil War and the first action of that war on Virginia's soil was an attack on Sewell's Point with no decisive result by two vessels from Old Point.

South of Craney Island is Portsmouth, where there has been a navy yard since Colonial days, the first one being built by the English, but utilized by the Virginians, after the departure of Lord Dunmure during the Revolution, for the building of the Virginia Navy. In 1801 it was purchased and transferred to the United States, being known as the Gosport Navy Yard. In April 1861 it was evacuated and burned and the ships sunk by the Union army. The Merrimac, which afterwards took so conspicuous a part in the war, was one of the ships sunk. She was raised, plated with iron (it is said according to models made by Commodore James Barron of Revolutionary fame), and renamed the Virginia, as she was always afterwards known by the Confederates. When they, in turn, on the advance of the Union army in May 1862, after the battle of the Monitor and Merrimac, evacuated the navy yard and the forts on Hampton Roads the Merrimac, or Virginia, was burned near Craney Island. After forty-five years her anchor has recently been recovered and may be seen at the Exposition. The present navy yard located partly in Portsmouth

THE RIP RAPS OR FORT WOOL

Hampton Roads

and partly in Norfolk is the largest in the United States, as is true also of the Naval Hospital near Portsmouth on whose site once stood Fort Nelson of Revolutionary times, later replaced by Fort Norfolk on the opposite shore.

The first white men who visited the site of Norfolk belonged to the expedition of Sir Walter Raleigh to Roanoke Island; while on a voyage of exploration as far as Chesapeake Bay some of its members found Indians on the Elizabeth River. But it was not until nearly one hundred years later, in 1682, that the city was founded, the original site of fifty acres being purchased for ten thousand pounds of tobacco. Almost another century passed before Portsmouth was settled in 1752. St. Paul's Church, which was built in Norfolk a few years before the settlement of Portsmouth, is one of the oldest buildings in the present city. Signs of very early Colonial occupation are to be found near Norfolk in Princess Anne County, where at Oceana still stands the little "Chapel by the Sea," built in 1680, and near Kempsville the ruins of "Old Hundred" chapel built in 1690. The silver service given to this church by Queen Anne is now in the Kempsville church, only ten years its junior. The name of a neighboring plantation, "Witchduck," recalls the fact that there in the days of the Salem persecution a young girl was drowned as a witch.

By 1770 Norfolk had grown to be the most populous and flourishing town in Virginia, Richmond being at that time a place of no significance. It was at the height of its Colonial prosperity, on New Year's Day 1776, that Norfolk was bombarded by Lord Dunmore, who had fled from Williamsburg after his dastardly robbing of the Powder Horn. Nearly fourteen hundred houses were destroyed at a loss of a million and a half dollars. One of the shells fired during the bombardment is still imbedded in a wall of St. Paul's Church.

After the Revolution Norfolk was rebuilt and increased rapidly in population and size. On the corner of Church and Main streets may still be seen in the pavement two marble footprints marking the spot where Lafayette stood when he addressed the people during his memorable visit in 1824. Within the last twenty years an old landmark has been destroyed—the "wishing oak" under which Powhatan's warriors smoked the peace pipe with neighboring tribes. It stood on the estate of Governor Tazewell, the site of the Hotel Lorraine. Two dates in the history of Norfolk stand out in the memory of her citizens—1855 when twenty-two hundred deaths occurred from yellow fever; and 1857 the year of the great freeze when, in January, passengers from New York went from Old Point to Norfolk on the ice. Richmond is now the largest and richest city in Virginia, but Norfolk is the second city in the state, being one of the most important shipping ports on the Atlantic seaboard.

III

OLD POINT COMFORT AND FORTRESS MONROE

IT was before the settlement of Jamestown that John Smith's band of adventurous colonists named the sandy strip of land at the eastern end of the Virginia peninsula "Point Comfort," on account of the good channel and safe anchorage it afforded. When later a similar strip at the mouth of Mobjack Bay received the name of New Point Comfort, the prefix "Old" naturally clung to the first. From the earliest times the strategic value of this point of land has been recognized and a fort was built upon it only two years after the landing at Jamestown. In 1609 Captain John Ratcliffe was sent down the river to fortify the point. "Algernoune Fort," when Don Diego Molina, a Spanish spy, saw it in 1611, consisted of stockades and posts without stone or brick and contained seven pieces of artillery, all of iron. It was manned by forty men. The name afterwards fell into disuse and the fort was referred to as Point Comfort Fort. It was rebuilt in 1630 and all newcomers to the Colony were ordered to pay sixty-four pounds of tobacco towards its maintenance. The garrison was paid in tobacco and corn, the captain receiving two thousand pounds of tobacco and ten barrels of corn. It was added to a third time in 1665 but was so inadequate as a defense that

Old Point Comfort and Fort Monroe

the Dutch twice in the seventeenth century invaded the harbor and burned the English shipping there. Finally in 1727 a new and larger fort was built of brick and named Fort George in honor of the reigning king. During the Revolution, just before the surrender at Yorktown, some additional fortifications were thrown up at Old Point Comfort by Count de Grasse, admiral of the French fleet.

After the War of 1812 it became evident that stronger fortifications were needed at Old Point Comfort and the matter began to be agitated by the Government. Five years after the war (1819) two acres on the Point were ceded to the Government. On this land the lighthouse now stands. The state made an additional cession to the Government in 1821 of two hundred and fifty acres, or all the land east and south of Mill Creek. A fort to enclose eighty acres was at once begun. It was medieval in character, with thick, high, granite walls surrounded by a broad and deep moat twenty-six acres in area and supplied with several drawbridges. Two hundred and fifty cannon were placed in deep embrasures, both in the main fort and in the water battery, and broad, grassy ramparts surmounted the casemates. The stone work was done by white masons but all other labor was performed by slaves hired at fifty cents a day from their masters. The fort, or more properly the fortress, since it is a fort within a fort, was named for President Monroe. The garrison numbered at first between three and five hundred men.

At the same time that Fort Monroe was begun, it was determined to add to the harbor defenses by mak-

Fort Monroe, Showing the Old Water Battery

Old Point Comfort and Fort Monroe

ing an artificial island on a shoal midway between Old Point Comfort and Sewell's Point opposite. The water here was fifteen feet deep and the making of the island was an immense task, necessitating the sinking of hundreds of thousands of tons of stone and the expenditure of millions of dollars. It was done, however, and then a small army of men was set to work to construct a fort of masonry similar to the one on the mainland, without the moat, but provided with large dark storerooms or dungeons built of solid masonry included within the walls. A rough railway was built around the island and huge derricks set up. The masonry work on Fort Wool, as the new fort was named, was still incomplete at the beginning of the Civil War, and although the construction proceeded for a time afterward, it soon became evident that with the rapid improvement in guns, powder, and projectiles, then in progress, parapets of masonry would no longer afford proper protection against naval attack. The massive granite walls of Fort Wool have lately been torn down, the old casemate batteries have been dismantled, and new batteries of rapid-firing guns have taken their place.

The War Department has recently proposed the construction of a second artificial island for the more complete defense of the harbor. This island is to be built upon shoals about midway between Cape Charles and Cape Henry and when completed will be strongly fortified. A sheltered harbor for vessels of war is to be provided. The total estimated cost of the new island, including fortifications and harbor, as submitted to Congress at its last session by the Secretary of War, is something over three millions of dollars.

Fort Monroe is the largest regular work of the kind in the United States and at the time of its completion in 1830 was considered proof against any possible attack by sea. Its masonry walls, moat, casemates, and interior constructions, still remain intact, but the old smooth-bore guns with their old-fashioned mounts have been removed, and the fort proper forms no part of the present system of harbor defenses. It is at present used to provide barracks and quarters for the regular artillery garrison of about one thousand men with their officers. The Artillery School for commissioned officers of the coast artillery is located at Fort Monroe, and all the junior officers, including graduates from the Military Academy at West Point, are required to take a special post-graduate course of study at this school in order to fit them for a proper performance of their professional duties. The walls of the old fort enclose a fine level parade ground, the scene of the daily guard mount and dress parade. It is ornamented by clumps of picturesque live-oaks, which do not grow further north than Old Point. The fort has received many distinguished guests and prisoners, and owns some interesting war trophies, such as the gun from the "Almirante Oquendo" captured during the battle of Santiago. It was at Fort Monroe that President Jefferson Davis was confined for a time after the dissolution of the Confederacy.

The artillery defenses of Hampton Roads and the entrance to Chesapeake Bay constitute a most important part of our system of National defense. In the

Old Point Comfort and Fort Monroe

event of war they must protect the Norfolk Navy Yard with its valuable naval base, also the shipping and vast commercial interests of the Chesapeake and, most important of all, they must make secure the water approaches to Washington and Baltimore. The heavy gun and mortar batteries which extend along the shore front just outside and to the north of Fort Monroe, are of the very latest and most formidable type. The big guns, mounted upon disappearing carriages, are placed behind thick parapets of solid concrete and sand which completely guard them from exposure to the enemy except at the instant of firing. Powerful searchlights are so placed along both sides of the main ship channel as to cross their beams and illumine the entire water areas within range of the guns for service at night. The fire from coast defense guns must be directed as effectively by night as by day, and in no other harbor are the preparations for defense against night attack so complete in every detail of equipment and drill.

Of considerable historic interest at Old Point Comfort was the old Hygeia Hotel, recently razed (1902) to make possible a military park. It had its beginning in a small house built in 1812 near the entrance to the Fort and consisting of one large room, which served for both parlor and dining-room, and four chambers on either side of it. The kitchen was in an outbuilding. This hostelry was later considerably enlarged but was finally removed in 1863 because it interfered with the training of guns in the fort. It was carted away entire across Mill Creek on a tram car drawn by fifty Government teams. The Hygeia was at once rebuilt

Old Point Comfort and Fort Monroe

on its later site close to the beach but was only a small rambling building. In 1874 Mr. Harrison Phoebus purchased it, fitted it with all the modern improvements, and added to it until it was large enough to accommodate twelve hundred guests. Every president of the United States except Mr. Cleveland has been entertained there, and among its guests have been numbered prominent foreign diplomats, admirals, army officers, statesmen, and financiers, among whom may be mentioned Jay Gould, King Kalakaua, and Li Hung Chang. The Chamberlain, with its sun galleries and winter gardens and its miles of promenades, has now superseded the Hygeia.

Between Old Point Comfort and Hampton is the National Soldiers' Home, which stands north of Mill Creek on the site of what was used during the war as the officers' division of the Hampton Hospital. Before the war its main building was used for the "Chesapeake Female College," having been built in 1854. The seminary did not have a long life and the building was afterwards used by a boy's school. In 1870 it was purchased for the Government, together with forty acres of land, by General B. F. Butler for $50,000 as a Home for disabled soldiers, to supplement the Homes already established in the North. Here live nearly four thousand veterans of the Mexican, Civil, and Spanish-American wars, who are given a home and medical attendance and are provided with two suits of clothes each year. The number of buildings has increased to nearly seventy and the Government has purchased forty-three acres of land in addition to the original forty. Everything possible is done for the

THE HYGEIA HOTEL

Photograph by Cheney, Hampton

Old Point Comfort and Fort Monroe

comfort and pleasure of the soldiers, the "post fund" derived from sales in the store, restaurant, and beer hall, providing from four to six monthly entertainments in the theatre and paying the expenses of a band, chapel, and library. Three large buildings have been erected for hospital purposes and are supplied with every modern appliance for the sick. Nearly 17,000 veterans have been cared for since the Home was established and about 9,000 of these now rest in the National Cemetery near by.

IV

OLD KECOUGHTAN

AT the end of the sixteenth century there stood somewhere near the shore of Hampton River an Indian village called Kecoughtan, said by Strachey in his History of Travaile into Virginia to have consisted of three hundred wigwams, sheltering a population of one thousand members of the Kecoughtan tribe.

These wigwams, which were in the form of huge ovens, were made by inserting saplings in the earth, their tops being afterward drawn to one point, in which position they were permanently kept by binding them together with withes. The framework was then covered with mats and pieces of bark. An opening was made in either side, and at the top was a place for the smoke to pass out from the fire of pine logs built on the earth in the centre of the wigwam. At night the beds were drawn in a circle about the fire, and "consisted of hurdles and reeds laid upon small poles, supported by posts rising only a foot from the ground." Upon these, mats and skins were placed, and the Indian in lying down would draw over him another mat or skin, using a third for a pillow. In the daytime when not hunting or fishing, the socially disposed Kecoughtan joined his neighbors on one of the scaffolds of reeds or dry willows which were built at intervals in

Old Kecoughtan

the village. Here the men smoked and conversed while the women spread maize and fish to dry on the lofts above.

The dress of these Indians was extremely simple, consisting mainly of skins ornamented with shells, bones, and teeth. They wore necklaces, ear-rings, and bracelets of birds' claws, bits of copper, and strings of pearls, feathers in their hair, and on their bodies paints of "lovely colors, beautiful and pleasing to the eye." Some were also tattooed with black and red "with little patches of lively colors in a braver fashion than those in the West Indies."

At meal time the Kecoughtan spread a mat on the ground and on this placed a dish of food. Before eating he took a small piece of food and threw it into the fire as an offering to the evil spirit, at the same time mumbling a sort of grace. The bill of fare varied with the season; in March and April the Indians depended on fish and game; in May they lived on strawberries, mulberries, oysters, and fish. During the summer they continued the fish and berry diet and added roasting ears, while in the fall and winter they counted on nuts, wild fowl, maize, and oysters. The principal root which they converted into food was the tuckahoe. This resembled the flag in its growth and was very abundant. In preparing it the Indians laid the roots in a pile and covered them with leaves, ferns, and earth. They then built a fire on either side which they allowed to burn for twenty-four hours. Old chroniclers tell us that the Indians grew fat or lean according to the season, but that actual famine was unknown.

The Kecoughtans are said to have been admirable

Old Kecoughtan

husbandmen ("better husbands then in any parte else that we have observed") and to have had as many as three thousand acres of cleared land, a large part of which was planted in maize. After clearing the land by the primitive method of girdling the trees, the ground was prepared for planting by means of a rude hoe made of a stick to which was attached the horn or shoulder-blade of a deer. Maize, beans, peas, pumpkins, gourds, and cymlins were planted in the same field. "A field of maize (near Kecoughtan) long before the vessels of the first English explorers appeared upon its waters, was almost the exact counterpart of the same field planted with the same grain three hundred years afterwards by the modern Virginia farmer.
* * * There would be the same number of stalks to the hill, with the vines of beans clambering upon the stalks, peas running over the ground between the rows, and pumpkins, bulky and yellow, peeping through the mass of green leaves." The grain was stored in long baskets in houses made especially for them.

The Indian garden was made near the wigwam and was from one to two hundred feet square. In it were grown muskmelons, gourds, and tobacco. In the autumn the Kecoughtans gathered great quantities of persimmons and after drying them stored them away like preserved dates or figs. The kernels of the chestnut and chinquapin were considered great delicacies when dried, beaten into flour, and converted into bread. The only salt in use in the village of Kecoughtan was the ash of stick-weed and hickory, and the Indians had no knowledge of any spirits except the juice of the crushed fiber of the maize stalk. Water gourds

AT THE MOUTH OF THE JAMES RIVER

Old Kecoughtan

were the flagons of the aboriginal Hamptonians. Partly on account of this abstinence and partly because of the active, out-of-door life led by all the tribe, the Kecoughtans in common with the other Virginia tribes were fine specimens of physical strength and grace. Their general health was good and they frequently lived to a great age.

The prosperity of the Kecoughtans excited the cupidity of Powhatan who, on the death of their old werowance when things were in confusion, attacked and conquered them. He made his son Pochins werowance and it was he and his warriors who, when Captain John Smith was exploring the shore near Point Comfort in his shallop, made signs to the white men to come ashore to their town whose bark-covered wigwams could be seen in the distance, and led the way by swimming across the river that lay between, the Englishmen following in their shallop. On reaching this village of the Kecoughtans (where the Soldiers' Home now stands) the strangers were hospitably entertained. Although at first received with "doleful noises," the occasion for which they did not understand, they were soon seated on mats and feasted till they could eat no more. When the meal was ended, they were given tobacco to smoke in huge clay pipes. We can imagine the curiosity with which the men from across the sea must have watched the strange, fantastic dance that formed part of their entertainment, and the interest with which they must have talked over their adventure with their shipmates on their return. Captain Smith describes the Indian town as located on a plain nearly surrounded by water. "Kecoughtan," he says, "so

Old Kecoughtan

conveniently turneth itself into Bayes and Creeks that it is a very pleasant place to inhabit, and is also a convenient harbor for fishing and other small boats." He found but eighteen wigwams instead of the three hundred mentioned by Strachey.

Not long after this adventure Captain Smith was sent by the starving colonists at Jamestown to Kecoughtan to trade for corn. The Indians, knowing the extremity of the English and looking on them with less friendly eyes since they had gained a footing in the land, held the corn at a high price, scorning the beads and other trinkets which were the usual medium of exchange. Smith, finally seeing that friendly overtures would not avail, decided to resort to force, and running his boat ashore he and his men shot off their muskets, whereat the Indians fled to the woods. As soon as the English landed, however, some sixty or seventy painted savages rushed back singing and dancing and bearing before them their "Okee" or idol which was made of painted skins stuffed with moss and loaded down with chains and ornaments of every description. They were armed with clubs, targets, and bows and arrows, but were unable to withstand the shot of the English and fled before them, leaving their god on the beach. This was immediately seized and held for ransom, the frightened Indians paying for the hideous object with boat-loads of venison, wild fowl, bread, oysters, and corn.

During the year that followed, the Indians seem to have grown accustomed to the presence of the English, and remembering no doubt with respect and admiration the prowess shown by the doughty captain on his

Old Kecoughtan

last visit, they entertained him right royally during the whole of Christmas week in 1608 when he was weatherbound at Kecoughtan. "The extreame wind, raine, frost, and snowe," says Captain Smith, "caused us to keep Christmas amongst the Savages; where wee were never more merrie, nor fedde on more plentie of good oysters, fish, flesh, wild foule, and good bread; nor never had better fires in England then in the drie, warme, smokie houses of Kecoughtan."

This pleasant picture of the red man's hospitality is the last that has come down to us. When next we hear of Pochins and his warriors, they have set upon and killed an Englishman, and for this offense Sir Thomas Gates has attacked and captured their town. This was in July 1610. To prevent the return of the Indians he built two forts, Charles and Henry, on the bank of the river, which he named Southampton in honor of the Earl of Southampton. This name was later contracted to Hampton. Corroborative testimony is borne to the situation of the forts at Kecoughtan by one Don Diego Molina, a Spanish spy taken prisoner at Point Comfort in 1613. In a letter to his government he speaks of two small forts, one of them garrisoned with fifteen soldiers, half a league distant from his prison at the Point.

When Sir Thomas Dale arrived from England in 1611 he found the settlers on Southampton River so improvident as to have neglected their spring planting and he set all hands to work sowing corn. Possibly they had grown indolent through the prodigality of Nature, for it is said that the colonists at Kecoughtan could live well with half the allowance the rest had

Old Kecoughtan

from the store because of the extraordinary quantity of fish and game there. Probably too the system of working in common which had been maintained up to this time had tended to paralyze industry. The alteration made by Sir Thomas Dale, who allotted to each man three acres of cleared ground requiring him to contribute two and a half barrels of corn to the public store, provided a new incentive to exertion and proved most beneficial. And so the little Colony became in time self-supporting and we hear nothing more of improvidence nor anything of its history until July 1619, when the House of Burgesses met for the first time at Jamestown. Among the famous requests sent by this body to King James was one which included a petition that the settlement on Southampton River should be relieved of the "heathen name" of Kecoughtan. A reply was received early in the following year granting the request and naming the whole of the lower peninsula, extending from Newport News and the Poquoson to Chesapeake Bay, for the king's daughter Elizabeth. Somewhat contracted the county remains to this day Elizabeth City, the town of Hampton taking its name from the river.

About twenty families formed the village at this time, the eleven farmers among them raising fine crops of tobacco and corn, beside cultivating peaches, apricots, and other fruits in large orchards. After the great massacre of 1622 the little village increased somewhat in size owing to additions from outlying plantations where the people feared to remain on account of the Indians. From all we can learn the town was never in such desperate straits as the neighboring

SHIRLEY ON THE JAMES

The First "Shirley" was a Place of Refuge in 1622

Photograph by Cook

Old Kecoughtan

settlement of Jamestown, and its subsequent growth would seem to justify the opinion of those historians who believe that the English would have been wiser had they made Kecoughtan their first Virginia settlement.

V

THE VIRGINIA PENINSULA IN THE SEVEN-
TEENTH CENTURY

THE end of the first decade of the seventeenth century found on the extreme eastern end of the Virginia peninsula, on the north shore of Hampton Roads, three small English settlements defended from the Indians by four forts. Settlers on arriving from England sometimes touched at Point Comfort where there was a tiny fortification named Fort Algernon—a collection of thatched cabins, one "slight house," and a store, the whole defended by seven pieces of artillery and a garrison of forty men. Two-thirds of a league farther on, at Kecoughtan, defended by the two small forts, Charles and Henry, the colonists found more comfortable quarters in which to rest after the long voyage; and then they proceeded to Jamestown or remained to plant maize and tobacco on the fertile farms bordering the Southampton (Hampton) River, from which Pochins, son of Powhatan, had lately been driven.

Life was easier at Kecoughtan than at Jamestown but the conditions were of the crudest. The scattered dwelling houses were chiefly cabins built of logs or slabs and carefully fortified by palisades. No man ventured into his fields, particularly after the massacre of 1622, without wearing a shirt of mail and carrying

COLONIAL CHURCH SILVER (1619)
Prayer Book Used at First Communion Service in America (June 21, 1607)

In the Seventeenth Century

firearms. Tobacco and sassafras were the chief exports but quantities of maize were raised and each colonist was compelled by law to plant annually for seven years six mulberry trees for the breeding of silkworms. The climate was believed to offer unusual advantages for silk culture and men skilled in that industry came from Europe and settled in Elizabeth City. French "vignerons" or vinedressers were imported and established themselves at Buckroe, where we find that land patents were granted as early as 1623, many French names occurring in the court records of that time. Neither of these industries, however, seems to have flourished for any length of time and the colonists settled down to ordinary agricultural pursuits, cultivating their plantations along the bay shore and on both sides of the river with the help of indentured white servants and a few black slaves.

Churches were built early in the history of every settlement but were at first only rough frame buildings that were later replaced by rectangular brick edifices, the walls of at least one of which still stand at Smithfield, Isle of Wight County. In the absence of towns the church became in a sense the centre of the social life of the county, although service was not held regularly and spiritual matters came to be sadly neglected in all the Virginia parishes. The Negroes were at first so few in number that no separate churches were built for them and they were permitted to attend the parish church, while their children were brought with others for baptism. The rules for the observance of the Sabbath were curiously strict. As early as Argall's time an edict was issued declaring that absence from

In the Seventeenth Century

church on Sundays or holidays should be punished by "confinement for the night and one week's slavery to the Colony, for the second offence the slavery should last a month, and for the third, for a year and a day." About the middle of the century a man of Poquoson Parish who was caught fishing on Sunday was compelled as a punishment to build a bridge for a public road.

The year 1634 is memorable for the establishment of the first successful free school in America. This was known as the Syms school and was situated on the Poquoson River in Elizabeth City County. Before the end of the century the Eaton free school was started at the head of Back River. After the Revolution a house was rented in Hampton and the two schools united under the name of the Hampton Academy. which eventually became part of the public school system.

Tutors were common in the better families of Virginia in the seventeenth century and the "parson's school" was a well-established institution. Masters were obliged to teach their bond apprentices to read and write and the law was enforced by the vestry under the general supervision of the county court. The following extract from the public records will show what was required:

July 18, 1698.   Elizabeth City County.

"Ann Chandler, orphan of Daniel Chandler, bound apprentice to Phyllemon Miller till 18 or day of marriage, to be taught to read a chapter in the Bible, ye Lord's Prayer and ten commandments, and semptress work."

In the Seventeenth Century

Elizabeth City was one of the eight boroughs into which the Colony was at first divided. In 1624 thirty persons were reported living at Buckroe and 319 in Elizabeth City including two Negroes; while eight years later we find that there were settlers at Fox Hill also. As the century advanced the typical mansion house of the landed proprietor came to be a frame building of moderate size with a chimney at each end and containing from six to twelve rooms. The partitions were covered with a thick layer of clay and then whitewashed with lime made from oyster shells. When bricks came into common use—having been made in the Colony and *not* brought from England—they were used in many cases instead of wood, and a few of these seventeenth century houses still stand on the peninsula. "Ringfield," the home of Joseph Ring of York County who died in 1703, is one of these. It was customary to fence in the garden with palings to keep out hogs and cattle, and the usual outbuildings including a dove-cot, stable, barn, henhouse, kitchen, milkhouse, and quarters for the servants, stood near the "Great House," the whole being surrounded by a high palisade. For although by a treaty in 1646 with Necotowance, the successor of Opechancanough, the Indians had ceded to the English all the territory between the York and the James from the Falls to Kecoughtan, and it was death for an Indian to be found in this territory unless as a messenger wearing a badge of striped cloth, yet the planters lived in continual fear of a new Indian massacre and took good care to bolt and bar doors and windows and to secure the gates of the stockade before retiring at night.

In the Seventeenth Century

Until the middle of the century there were but few black slaves compared with the number of white servants. In 1672 the population had reached 40,000, of whom 6,000 were indentured servants while only one-third as many were slaves. A few Indians were enslaved but were never so valuable as the Negroes, one of the latter bringing 4,500 pounds of tobacco while an Indian was worth but 3,000 pounds. Later the price of an adult Negro slave in Elizabeth City County was about twenty-five pounds sterling.

Nails and hinges were very scarce throughout the Colony and gates were therefore not usual, draw-bars such as are still common in Virginia being used where they were needed in the rail fences. Travel was done mostly on horseback, the roads being often mere bridal paths, or when wider being so much worse than the proverbially bad Virginia roads of the present time as to be almost impassable for carriages. In 1662 an Act of Assembly was passed ordering roads forty feet wide to be made, "one to the church, one to the courthouse at Jamestown, and one from county to county." There was a ferry across the mouth of the Southampton River, the ferryman being granted the privilege of running it for life on condition that he charged but one penny for the transportation of each passenger.

After the colonists had somewhat recovered from the disorganization caused by the events which culminated in Bacon's Rebellion, one of the first things that engaged their attention was the establishment of towns for storehouses of tobacco. In 1680 in each county fifty acres of land were purchased by the public officers and all persons were encouraged to settle on

The Oldest Custom House in America
(See Page 96)

Photograph by Cook

In the Seventeenth Century

this land who would build a dwelling and warehouse thereupon, each such person being assigned half an acre of land in fee simple for which he was to pay to the county one hundred pounds of tobacco. In Elizabeth City County the plot purchased was on the west side of the river on a plantation belonging to one Thomas Jervise and the price paid was 10,000 pounds of tobacco. This was undoubtedly the reason for the establishment of the present town of Hampton on the west side of the river. By 1698 the place had become of sufficient importance to require a special constable and in 1705 it was legally incorporated as a town.

The last decade of the seventeenth century was marked by great prosperity. The Rev. James Blair had been appointed Commissary of Virginia and had assumed supervision of the churches, thus becoming the nearest approach to a bishop that the Episcopal Church in America had for two hundred years. At his suggestion the Assembly now entered heartily into the plan suggested as early as 1619 for establishing a college in the Colony, and in 1692 "William and Mary" received her charter "to educate young men to be ministers of the Gospel and to propagate the Christian faith among the Western Indians." Its first Commencement was held in 1700 and must have been an interesting occasion, for there were present not only the aristocratic families of Williamsburg, now the capital of the Colony, but planters and their families from every part of the peninsula arrived by boat or coach, while the river was filled with sloops from New York, Pennsylvania, and Maryland. The Indians, too, came in to see the spectacle and must have added picturesqueness to the scene. Brafferton Hall in the college yard

In the Seventeenth Century

was set apart for a day school for Indians but only a few ever availed themselves of these educational privileges and the attendance was increased by boys from the town. The course of study consisted of "reading, writing, and vulgar arithmetic."

It was in the third year of this decade that the first post-office in Virginia was established by Governor Nicholson. There was a central office at the capital and one in each county; the postage for one sheet of paper was three cents for a distance not exceeding eighty miles. At this time the largest personal property inventoried in Elizabeth City County in a single case was worth two hundred and eighty-two pounds sterling. The average value of the land was a quarter of a pound sterling per acre, while in York County it was worth twice as much and in the newer counties much less.

Besides the planters in Virginia there were tanners, shoemakers, millers, vinedressers, and pitch and tar makers. The people had their churches and free schools, a college, plenty of land, many servants, abundance of fish and game, and a free market in England and the other colonies for their surplus products. The Indians were far beyond their borders and although pirates infected the seas their depredations were not so much felt as they were on the Carolina coast. The isolated life on the plantations had developed self-reliance and other manly qualities, together with a love of liberty which had already shown itself in both church and state affairs. The Virginia gentleman could look back on a century of adventure, enterprise, and growth. In secular matters, at least, the Colony was at the height of its prosperity.

THE HISTORIC NELSON MANSION, YORKTOWN
Built Early in the Eighteenth Century

VI
PIRATES OF THE VIRGINIA CAPES

THE seventeenth century was the golden age of piracy in America—a period which produced the most famous buccaneers of history, and whose annals are full of desperate encounters on the high seas which always ended in the triumph of the black flag. There is not much doubt that the English Navigation Acts were responsible for the encouragement of piracy by the early colonies. It is not to be wondered at that when the colonists discovered that they could neither buy nor sell save in an English market which set its own prices, they should have become quite willing to tolerate the lawless traders who could afford to sell for a song what had cost them only hard blows. Neither was it strange that with such encouragement the pirates should have rapidly become bolder and have extended their operations along the whole Atlantic coast.

The history of this time is filled with accounts on the one hand of the efforts of the colonists to evade the navigation laws and on the other of the struggles of the home government to enforce the laws against pirates. Charles Town in South Carolina was a favorite resort of the robbers of the sea,

Pirates of the Virginia Capes

and although their welcome varied in warmth from time to time, yet until the last decade of the century piratical vessels found safe anchorage in Charles Town harbor or in the inlets and coves along the coast. During the closing years of the century, however, a rapid change came over public opinion in South Carolina regarding piracy, and Charles Town strung up pirates at the entrance of her harbor, scarcely waiting to hurry through a formal trial. But driven from South Carolina by the enforcement of severe laws, the sea-robbers harried the North Carolina coast and were concealed and befriended by some of the highest officials.

From the new rendezvous they made expeditions to the Virginia capes and even to the New England coast. In the year 1700 a piratical vessel was seen between Cape Charles and Cape Henry and reported to the Shoreham, a fifth-rate man-of-war lying in Hampton Roads. Governor Nicholson chanced to be at Kecoughtan at the time, and hearing the news went on board the Shoreham and was present at the engagement between the ships which resulted in the surrender of the pirate. One is carried back in imagination to that eventful twenty-ninth of April 1700 by the epitaph still to be seen on a flat black slab on Pembroke Farm near Hampton—the site of one of the early churches —to the memory of the gallant Peter Heyman: "This stone was given by His Excellency, Francis Nicholson, Esq., Lieutenant and Governor-General of Virginia, in memory of Peter Heyman, Esq.,

Pirates of the Virginia Capes

grandson to Sir Peter Heyman of Summerfield in ye county of Kent—he was collector of customs in ye lower district of James River and went voluntarily on board ye king's ship Shoreham in pursuit of a pyrate who greatly infested this coast—after he had behaved himself 7 hrs. with undaunted courage, was killed with a small shot, ye 29 day of April 1700. In the engagement he stood next the Governor upon the quarter deck, and was here honorably interred by his order."

Early in 1717 a notorious sea-robber by the name of Stede Bonnet—a wealthy man of Barbadoes who had been driven by an unhappy marriage into the "humour of going a pyrating"—made his first cruise off the capes of Virginia, in a sloop called the Revenge, and captured a number of merchant vessels, plundering and burning them and sending their crews ashore. He led an adventurous life filled with all manner of crimes, desperate sea-fights, and hair-breadth escapes, and was finally executed at Charles Town after one of the most famous trials in the history of the Colony.

On one of his cruises Bonnet fell in with another famous pirate—perhaps the most disreputable that ever lived—whose name has always been associated with Virginia, albeit more on account of the grewsome trophy which a brave soldier forced him to contribute to the Colony than for any desperate or bloody deeds committed against the Virginians. Blackbeard must have been a revolting monster in appearance; in fact his ambition was to resemble the devil as closely as possible. He received his name from the fact that he wore a black beard of extraordinary length which he also allowed to grow

Pirates of the Virginia Capes

entirely up to his eyes. He was in the habit of twisting it with ribbons into small tails and turning them up about his ears. When about to engage in a fight he would stick lighted matches under his hat on each side of his face and so make himself look like the real demon that he was. He wore a sling over his shoulders in which he carried three brace of pistols hanging in holsters.

But even this wild sea-robber had occasional longings for a quieter life, for he took advantage of the proclamation of George the First offering pardon to all pirates who would surrender themselves within a year, and gave himself up to Governor Eden of N. C., taking the oath of allegiance to the Crown. It was while living thus in "respectable" idleness that he took unto himself his thirteenth wife—a young girl of sixteen! The attractions of the old life proved too strong for Blackbeard however and after a few months he went to sea again under the black flag. In the Bay of Honduras he met Stede Bonnet and joined forces with him, but soon discovering that the gentleman from Barbadoes knew nothing of seamanship and was held in contempt by his crew, Blackbeard coolly deposed him, gave him a subordinate position on another vessel, added the Revenge to his own fleet, and making Ocracoke Inlet in North Carolina his headquarters, again spread terror along the coast. After committing several piracies near the Virginia capes he appeared once more before Charles Town, captured all outgoing merchant vessels, and imprisoned a number of its dis-

Pirates of the Virginia Capes

tinguished citizens, using them to enforce the most outrageous demands on the town. He then sailed back to his headquarters and after taking a number of prizes shared his plunder with Governor Eden, thus, securing immunity from punishment.

The North Carolina planters now became so exasperated by Blackbeard's depredations that they determined to be rid of him, and knowing that they could hope for no redress from their own governor they applied to Governor Spottswood of Virginia for assistance, which was promptly given. A proclamation was at once issued placing a price on the head of Blackbeard, and officers were dispatched in command of two sloops to bring the outlaw to Virginia, dead or alive. All the world knows the story of Lieutenant Maynard's brave fight on the deck of his sloop in the shallow waters of Ocracoke Inlet when twelve of his men were killed and twenty-two wounded, while he himself engaged Blackbeard in a fierce, hand-to-hand struggle which finally ended in the pirate's death after he had received twenty-five wounds. With Blackbeard's head nailed to his bowsprit and fifteen of the pirate crew in irons Maynard sailed back in triumph between the Virginia capes. Tradition says that the pirate's head was exposed on a pole at the end of a sandy point on the west side of Hampton River. The spot is known to this day as "Blackbeard's Point" and the place near Williamsburg where thirteen of Maynard's prisoners were hung is still called "Pirates' Road."

It is a curious fact, recently discovered, and attested in the valuable monograph on "The Carolina Pirates and Colonial Commerce" issued by Johns Hopkins University, that although Blackbeard was known as Ned Teach or Thatch of Bristol, his real name was Drummond as vouched for by "one of his own family and name, of respectable standing, in Virginia near Hampton." It is the more curious because the old mansion house directly opposite Blackbeard's Point was owned for many years by a branch of the Drummond family, possibly distant connections of the famous freebooter.

It is not strange perhaps that various ballads should have been written about the notorious Blackbeard, certainly not that his story should have appealed to a boy of thirteen fond of scribbling verses. Edward Everett Hale tells us in the *New England Magazine* for June 1898 that he discovered in a recently published volume called "Real Sea Songs" a ballad about Blackbeard written by Benjamin Franklin when he was thirteen.

VII

THE VIRGINIA PENINSULA IN THE EIGHTEENTH CENTURY

THE luxurious manner of living begun in the Virginia Colony in the last decade of the seventeenth century continued for more than half of the eighteenth. The pioneer with firearms became "a ruffled dignitary riding in his coach and four;" log huts and unpretentious brick dwellings gave place to fine manor houses; forests disappeared and were replaced by cultivated plantations; the number of tobacco fields increased and with them the number of black slaves; the tobacco was carried to England and the ships returned laden with rich cargoes, to discharge their treasures at their owners' wharves. It was a leisurely time. The men were deliberate both in work and pleasure; they lingered over their wine and their pipes; they drove or rode long distances with their families to the plantations of their friends and remained for extended visits. The women rode to hounds with the men and were as much at home on the water as on land, handling a tiller or trimming a sail as skillfully as their brothers.

Many of the planters gathered in the capital during the winter, and in the *Virginia Gazette* of that period we find announcements of their pleas-

In the Eighteenth Century

ures. "This evening will be performed," we read, "by the young Gentlemen of the College, the Tragedy of Cato." * * * "Last Saturday being His Majesty's birthday, the same was observed here with firing of guns, illuminations and other demonstrations of loyalty, and at night there was a handsome appearance of Gentlemen and Ladies at His Honour the Governor's, where was a Ball and an Elegant Entertainment." That this was not the way "the other half" lived is shown by sundry advertisements and notices. Two Negro men—runaway slaves—are advertised for; two others are hanged for robbery; a Negro woman is burned for killing her mistress; an Indian servant has committed a misdemeanor; and down in Princess Anne County a "witch" is ducked. Yet on the whole it was a marvellously happy and picturesque age. The slaves were, as a rule, well treated and they were devoted to their masters' interests. Lower down on the peninsula the plantations were small and the slaves few in number. The 'longshoremen lived by their nets and the small landholders by their farms. Hampton was a port of entry as well as a shipping port for tobacco and there was consequently much business in the way of customs and tonnage duties. In fact it was the place of greatest trade in Virginia and was also the county seat, with courthouse and prison (built in 1716), pillory, whipping-post, and ducking-stool. There were then no telegraphs, railways, or electric lights. In 1710 a postal service was established that carried letters once a fortnight from

CARTER'S GROVE, JAMES RIVER
Built by "King" Carter About 1730

In the Eighteenth Century

Williamsburg to Philadelphia, but it was not till twenty years later that through the efforts of Governor Spottswood, then Postmaster-General for the American Colonies, a regular mail service was started between New England and the James River. The time from Philadelphia to Williamsburg was reduced to one week, but for points further South the post-rider did not start until enough mail had accumulated to make the journey worth while!

This same Governor Spottswood was perhaps the most picturesque figure of this picturesque age. He arrived in Virginia just one hundred years after Lord De la Warre built the two forts on Hampton River to protect the infant town of Kecoughtan. He is remembered as one of the best of the Colonial governors, known far beyond the borders of Virginia for his energy and love of justice. We have an interesting glimpse of the Indians of Tidewater, Virginia, when we read of Spottswood's visit in 1716 to his mission school at Fort Christanna. "Here," says John Esten Cook, "there were seventy-seven Indian children at school. They were taught to write and to read the Bible and prayerbook. Sixty youths were present (at the time of the Governor's visit) with feathers in their hair and ears; their faces painted with blue and vermilion; and with blue and red blankets around their shoulders." In the same year that the Governor visited his Indian mission he led a gallant expedition of Virginia cavaliers into the mountains that formed the western boundary of the province.

In the Eighteenth Century

From the time that the spirited soldier-governor thus founded the order of the "Knights of the Golden Horseshoe" until his death at Temple Farm near Yorktown in 1740, his life was one of great activity and usefulness. Now we hear him asking his Burgesses why they continue to sit day after day and draw their pay for doing nothing if the country is too poor, as they claim, to carry out needed measures for the public good. Later we look on with mingled amusement and regret when he is worsted in his quarrel with Commissary Blair and obliged to retire from office. Again we read with warm interest the story of his happy family life in the "enchanted castle" at Germanna, as told by Colonel William Byrd of Westover. Governor Spottswood was buried at Temple Farm, the former name of the Moore House, where in 1781 the Revolution came to an end with the signing of the articles of capitulation by Lord Cornwallis.

In 1716 Hampton was a place of one hundred houses and the people lived in great comfort. There was at this time however no church in the village, service being held in the courthouse. The first church appears to have stood on the east side of Hampton River. The first minister was the Rev. Wm. Mease who is said to have come to Virginia with Sir Thomas Gates in 1610. The glebe land was also on the east side of the river, as well as the common land of fifteen hundred acres and the company's land of three thousand acres. Here, near the "Indian House Thicket" was leased a piece

AN EIGHTEENTH CENTURY MANOR HOUSE
The Home of the President of William and Mary College

In the Eighteenth Century

of land by one of the early ministers of this parish who, says Lyon G. Tyler in his Cradle of the Republic, was the first exponent of the idea that "the only good Indian is a dead Indian," having published a letter expressing his belief that it would be useless to attempt to civilize the Indians until their head men were put to death. It is a curious coincidence that Hampton Institute, which has helped to prove the falsity of the minister's position by training hundreds of Indians for useful citizenship, should stand, as it does, so near the spot formerly leased by this "man of little faith." About the middle of the seventeenth century a new church was built at Pembroke Farm, one mile west of Hampton, where four ancient tombstones still mark its site. It was because this church was out repair that from 1694 to 1728, when the foundations of old St. John's were dug, services were held in the courthouse, first in the old one and then in the new one built in 1716.

St. John's Church, then, one of the oldest now in use in the United States, dates from 1728 when it was built of bricks burned with wood taken "from the School land"—the "School" being the one established by Benjamin Syms, the first free school in America. The bricks were called "English" but it was because they were made in English moulds and not because they were brought from England. Bricks of the same kind are found in the Jamestown tower, in St. Luke's (1632) at Smithfield, in St. Paul's (1739), Norfolk, and in other early Colonial churches. One of the rectors

In the Eighteenth Century

of St. John's writes to the Bishop of London sometime between 1719 and 1731 that his parish is fifty miles in circumference and contains three hundred and fifty families, that there are about one hundred communicants, and that the slave owners are careful to instruct the young Negro children and bring them to baptism. In 1760 one of the parishioners bequeathed forty pounds sterling towards purchasing a bell "out of England," provided the vestry and church wardens would undertake to build the belfry within twelve months. The old vestry book (dating back to 1751) tells of the contracts awarded for building and painting the belfry, and no doubt the bell was purchased, for later records speak of the "old Queen Anne bell which hung in the tower on the west end of the church."

Since the middle of the seventeenth century Elizabeth City Parish has been in possession of the oldest and most precious communion silver belonging to the Episcopal Church in America—a cup, chalice, and paten brought to Virginia in 1619. They were the gift of one Mistress Robinson in England to the church at Smith's (afterward Southampton) Hundred, which was destroyed during the Indian massacre of 1622. The silver was preserved by Governor Yeardley and after his death was kept at Jamestown, being finally transferred to Hampton, probably because the place was named for the same Earl of Southampton who gave his name to Smith's Hundred. They have survived three wars and at least three great fires.

By the middle of the eighteenth century the end

St. John's Church, Hampton

Photograph by Cheney

In the Eighteenth Century

of the Colonial period was in sight. The free life of the new world had created new modes of thought, and old ideas of government began to be seriously questioned. Democracy became popular and the idea of uniting for resistance to the demands of the mother country began to agitate the colonies. Aristocratic Virginia sounded the alarm and it was her sons who were the great leaders of the Revolution—Patrick Henry, Jefferson, Mason, Washington, Lee, Pendleton, and a host of others. Among them was George Wythe, a native of Elizabeth City County, whose home at "Chesterville" still stands. He was an eminent jurist, Chancellor of Virginia for more than twenty years, and one of the signers of the Declaration of Independence.

VIII

THE VIKINGS OF VIRGINIA

THE progress of revolutionary thought in the American Colonies during the latter half of the eighteenth century is well known. Every school boy has his Revolutionary hero and knows by heart the celebrated speeches of the famous Virginian leaders. What American has not followed with breathless interest the stirring history of his country's struggle for independence? Who has not kept pace with Jefferson's thought from the time he listened—a young law student—outside the door as Patrick Henry thundered against the right of the mother country to vest the power of taxation in any other body than the Colonial Assembly, ending with the famous words, "If this be treason, make the most of it," to that other time more than ten years later when he drafted the Declaration of Independence which transformed Englishmen into Americans? Who has not wintered with Washington in Valley Forge and exulted with him at Yorktown and been proud to honor his memory as the Father of his Country? But familiar as is the story of the Revolution, there is one chapter that has often been omitted, and it is one that is intimately connected with the history of the lower Virginia peninsula—the record of the gallant

The Vikings of Virginia

State Navy that did such honorable service in the bays and creeks and rivers of Tidewater Virginia.

By the winter of 1774 Virginia was under arms, a company of militia having been formed in every county, ready on Washington's order to march at a minute's notice. In the spring was fought in Massachusetts the battle of Lexington, and the very next day the haughty Lord Dunmore—"the worst governor Virginia ever had"—secretly ordered the gunpowder stored in the magazine at Williamsburg to be carried on board the man-of-war Magdalen then lying in James River. This act threw Virginia into commotion and called out the minute-men, obliging Dunmore to leave the dangerous little capital. The state being without an executive and Washington having been called to take command of the Continental Army, a Committee of Safety was appointed in Virginia with Edmund Pendleton as Chairman. Patrick Henry was chosen commander-in-chief of the Virginia forces. His famous militia carried for their flag a picture of a rattlesnake with the words, "Don't Tread on Me," and the men wore green hunting shirts bearing the words "Liberty or Death;" it is said that they carried tomahawks and scalping knives in their belts and wore buck tails in their caps. Dunmore in his wrath offered freedom to all slaves who would join the King's party, and sailed with his royalist friends to the shores of the Chesapeake and the rivers that make into the lower peninsula, ravaging plantations and laying waste the country. Elizabeth City County was espe-

The Vikings of Virginia

cially exposed to his attacks and to those of British privateers. Many homes were burned to the ground, crops were destroyed, and slaves were carried off to the West Indies. Dunmore's last act was to bombard the city of Norfolk and burn it to the ground. The whole country was aroused and the Committee of Safety was authorized to procure armed vessels for the protection of the coast.

In April 1776 there appeared in the *Virginia Gazette* a call for ships' carpenters and the building of the Virginia Navy went on apace. Many of the ships were built at Hampton, some in Norfolk, some in Accomac, some at the shipyard on the Chickahominy. Others belonged to the merchant marine and were purchased and armed for the state service, the new rigging having always "the rogue's yarn" to distinguish it from that of the merchant ships. For "a hundred wild sea-blown years" had adventurers, pirates, and sea captains sailed their ships up and down the Chesapeake and in and out among its sinuous waterways; fishermen lined the shores and had explored in their canoes every inlet and cove; it was not difficult therefore to man the new ships with watermen of every description, only too eager to chase the privateers and to defend their homes. They became the Vikings of Virginia, darting hither and thither in their fast-sailing craft and surprising and capturing many a plunder-laden ship.

A Board of Naval Commissioners was appointed in May 1776 to direct the affairs of the navy, and by midsummer a fleet of seventy vessels was in

St. Paul's Church, Norfolk

At the Extreme Right is the Revolutionary Cannon Ball

Photograph by Cook of Richmond

The Vikings of Virginia

commission. It was rightly called a "mosquito fleet," for the vessels were all small, and they were probably the fastest sailers in the world—except the lateens of the Mediterranean. Then they were of such light draught that they were perfectly at home in the shallow inlets, where they gave the enemy many a sting that was long remembered. The fleet included frigates, brigs, brigantines, schooners, sloops, galleys, and armed pilot boats and barges. Some were row-galleys, one-half decked over and provided with high and strong bulwarks. These galleys looked like huge water spiders, being broad and flat and usually rigged as schooners with two or three masts. They were used as "lookouts" or flying sentinels as well as for transports for troops, each being large enough to carry a company of sixty-eight men with arms and baggage. The average length of deck was seventy feet and they were heavily armed, carrying two twenty-four or thirty-two pounders in bow and stern and seven smaller guns along each side. The largest ships carried thirty-two guns each; one of them—the Gloucester—was a prison ship and was moored in Hampton Creek or in Elizabeth River. The ships of the Virginia Navy sailed as fleets on only two occasions, once in Hampton Roads to give help to the troops in Portsmouth and once in James River. In each case the fleet consisted of fourteen ships. As Virginia had no distinctive state flag it is probable that Patrick Henry's famous banner was used in the navy. Only one of the Virginia ships survived the war—the gallant Liberty—which fought in twenty distinct actions and was twice sunk in the rivers. Instead of being retained by the state, as she should have been, she was sold to a trader in the West Indies.

Of all the brave and dashing Virginia Vikings, Commodore James Barron of Hampton was doubtless the master spirit. He was born in 1740 when his father, Captain Barron, was Commander of Fort George at Old Point Comfort. Here he lived for nine years, when a hurricane destroyed the fortifications and the family moved further up the peninsula. The boy James began his sea life when he was but ten years old; he soon became second mate and later was given command of a small vessel, the Kecoughtan. He and his brother, Richard Barron, became pilots and with their swift boats gave Governor Dunmore and his Tory friends much trouble. On one occasion, before the formation of the State Navy, they were chased into Hampton by the British schooner Otter which however ran aground. They immediately attacked and burned her, the crew escaping. In revenge for this act, angry Captain Squires appeared in Hampton Creek with six armed sloops and made an attack on the town. But the townspeople, anticipating this, had applied for help to the Committee of Safety. One hundred Culpeper minute-men responded and with the Hampton militia, among whom was James Barron, concealed themselves behind bushes and houses and made a fierce resistance, sinking or destroying five of the sloops. It was in the summer of the following year that the

The Vikings of Virginia

Virginia Navy was organized and Hampton was not again attacked by the British.

The story of the "web-footed Barrons" would almost make a naval history. James Barron the elder was made one of the three commodores of the State Navy and in 1779 became senior officer, receiving his commission as "commander-in-chief of all the armed forces of the Commonwealth" from Colonel Thomas Whiting of Hampton who was President of the Naval Board.* Commodore Barron rendered Virginia valuable service during the Revolutionary War, not only in his official capacity but by loaning money and stores and by aiding in procuring supplies for the army, particularly during the siege of Yorktown. He served with his brother, Captain Richard Barron, during the whole war, commanding the famous ship Liberty in many gallant fights. The Patriot which also has an interesting history was commanded by Captain Richard Barron for at least a portion of the time. The two sons of Commodore James Barron, James, the younger, and Samuel, were both attached to the State Navy, and afterwards won distinction in the United States Navy, both becoming commodores and being conspicuous for their bravery and for their executive ability.

Lieutenant Cunningham of the Virginia Navy, who when a prisoner in Portsmouth made such a daring and romantic escape, running the guard and

---

* This commission, signed by Jefferson, is now in possession of Mrs. Janie Hope Marr of Lexington, Va., one of the descendants of Commodore Barron.

swimming the river to join his wife in the woods on the other side, was also a native of Hampton.

No official record has been kept of the exploits of the State Navy, but we find scattered reports here and there of daring feats and successful captures. The movements of the ships were not confined to the Roads or to the Bay, for we read that in September 1776 six ships were ordered to the West Indies to buy supplies; and more than once their battles were fought outside the capes. In June 1776 the Barron brothers seized the Oxford, a British transport, off the capes, taking prisoners two hundred and seventeen Highland soldiers; and in July Captain Richard Barron captured in the same place a Tory sloop from the West Indies and a large brig carrying provisions from England. Again, we read of a son of Commodore James Barron (Captain Sam Barron), who distinguished himself in an action with an enemy's vessel in Hampton Creek. When the enemy surrendered, it was found that more British were killed and wounded than there were Americans on the Virginia vessel. In 1779, however, a British fleet appeared in Hampton Roads and captured a large number of American vessels, the smaller ones retiring to the shallow bays and rivers. Later, in 1781, the roadstead was again in possession of a British fleet filled with Cornwallis's army, which had just evacuated Portsmouth. In May of this year one of the little Virginia vessels successfully eluded the whole of the British fleet, passing directly through it under cover of night. It was probably about this time that the

The Vikings of Virginia

last fight of the Patriot was witnessed by three loyal friends, Captain Mark Starlin and two of the Barrons, who were lying in the woods on the north shore of James River watching for a boat to take them across, when to their great joy they saw the plucky little Patriot, sailed by a Captain Watkins, chasing an English ship up the river. It was but a ruse of the British, however, who suddenly turned and gave battle, capturing the little vessel. Captain Starlin was an African slave but commanded his own boat and was given authority equal to that of other officers of the same rank. A number of other black seamen helped to man the Virginia navy.

While the army of Cornwallis was occupying Hampton Roads, foraging parties were landed daily on James River and were often discovered and given battle by the local militia. Colonel Francis Mallory of Hampton took an active part in these skirmishes and was at one time taken prisoner and held on board one of the ships of the British fleet. His brother, Captain Edward Mallory, tried in vain to secure his release until he succeeded in making prisoner a certain Captain Brown who had been out for provisions. This officer was exchanged for Colonel Mallory but was so severely wounded that he died before he could be removed to his ship. Although he had been warned not to take up arms against the British again, Colonel Mallory was soon at his old work and met a force of four hundred British soldiers with forty of his militia at the bridge connecting

The Vikings of Virginia

York and Elizabeth City counties. The Americans made a stubborn resistance against overwhelming numbers, and the enemy, recognizing Mallory, who had refused a chance to escape, shot him down and ran him through with their bayonets. His buff vest, which was preserved by his family, was pierced by eleven bayonet holes.

When Cornwallis surrendered at Yorktown, not a vestige of the Virginia Navy remained except the Liberty. Commodore Barron retired to his home at Hampton but, hearing that an English privateer had captured a Baltimore vessel bound to Hampton, true to his Viking spirit he hastily collected twenty of his old associates, manned a schooner, and gave chase to the Englishman, recapturing the Baltimore vessel. "As long as there was a plank to stand on or a flag to follow" he fought for the cause of his country's liberty—a worthy representative of an illustrious family.

IX

HAMPTON IN THREE WARS

DURING the century between 1770 and 1870 the little town of Hampton was visited by three wars. Owing to the numerous arms of the sea that indent the coast of eastern Virginia, Hampton and the outlying plantations were peculiarly exposed to attacks by sea, and during the Revolutionary period so great was the danger from this source that the gallant little State Navy was organized, as we have seen, for coast defense. Skirmishes between the militia and detachments from Dunmore's and Cornwallis's fleets in the Roads, continued during the whole period of the war, but after the repulse of Captain ' Squire's force in 1775 there was no attack on Hampton during the Revolution.

Tradition says that in 1776, shortly after the declaration of independence, the steeple of St. John's Church was struck by lightning and the royal coat of arms which had adorned it was thrown to the ground. However that may be, the people certainly threw off the English yoke and made a stand for democratic equality. The change was apparent not only in government affairs but in social and domestic matters. Simplicity of dress became the rule, ceremony and pomp in public functions were discarded, class distinctions became weaker, and the great plantations dwindled in size. Fortunately the old English love of outdoor life and sports, and the cordiality and hospitality of his ancestors, remained to the Virginian; and hunting, fishing, fox hunting, and the entertainment of guests are still the chief pleasures of the residents of Tidewater Virginia.

The War of 1812 was more destructive than the Revolution in its effect on the town of Hampton. Admiral Cockburn, who commanded a British fleet lying in the Roads, made an attack on Hampton June 25, 1813. Landing a force of 2,500 men at what is now "Indian River," he himself sailed with a small fleet towards Hampton Creek, appearing off Blackbeard's Point from whence he shelled the town. The water front was protected by seven small guns and four hundred and fifty militia who were encamped at "Little England" farm (now known as West End) under command of Colonel Crutchfield. The little garrison repulsed the enemy for a time, but the latter, joining the land party, obliged Colonel Crutchfield's force to retreat up the peninsula, in which direction many of the inhabitants had already fled. The outrages permitted by the British during their two days' stay have made this occupation of Hampton notorious in history. The town was given up to pillage and the inhabitants assaulted and robbed. This vandalism is attributed to the French prisoners, who formed part of the British force and were fresh from similar scenes of plunder and outrage in Spain.

St. John's at the Close of the Civil War

Hampton in Three Wars

Mr. Richard B. Servant, who was for many years secretary of the vestry of St. John's Church, says that when he came into town, a boy of twelve, after the British had evacuated it in 1813, he found that they had used the old graveyard as a slaughter house for cattle and that the church walls bore marks of fires that the soldiers had kindled to cook their meals. The interior of the church had been used as a common barrack. Just before the war the old Queen Anne bell of the parish had been removed to the militia camp at "Little England." The tongue had become loose and an axe that had been used to strike the hour and cracked the famous old bell. From this time to 1824 the church was allowed to go to decay and became a common shelter for horses, cattle, and hogs. Religion must have been at a low ebb indeed to have allowed such desecration of a sacred edifice in time of peace. It is said that when efforts were finally made to restore the church, it was difficult to find more than a half-dozen prayerbooks in the parish. The first suggestion to restore the church property to its former condition was made in 1822 or 1823 by Mrs. Jane Hope, the eldest daughter of Commodore James Barron. Her suggestion was acted upon by Mr. Servant who succeeded in raising funds to rebuild the walls of the graveyard and to place a wrought-iron gate at the entrance. A meeting of the friends of the church followed and a vestry was elected, the members of which made a determined effort to raise funds for the repair of the church. At this time nothing was standing but

Hampton in Three Wars

bare walls and a leaky roof; nothing else remained but the English tiles on the floor, all the church furniture having been destroyed. Fortunately the vestry book had been carefully preserved by a resident and is still intact, a moth-eaten, crumbling volume containing the parish records since 1751. The church enclosure was cleaned and occasional services held while the repairs were going on, some of the worshipers sitting on the bare tiles of the floor. Early in 1830 these repairs were completed and the church was consecrated by Bishop Moore. The old bell was recast and remained for many years the best bell in the country.

For thirty-one years the parish records of St. John's continue unbroken; then again, in 1861, all but the walls and the vestry book are sacrificed. On a midsummer night, in order to prevent its occupation by Federal troops, Hampton was fired by the property owners of the town—officers and soldiers in the Confederate army—"to demonstrate the intense earnestness of the people in the cause they had espoused and for which they considered no sacrifice too great." But five houses and the church walls remained standing on the site of the attractive little village of Hampton. Only one of these houses is now standing. There were but few people in the town and these were notified of the plans of General Magruder, the commanding officer, who had reluctantly yielded to the wishes of the inhabitants to destroy their two hundred thousand dollars' worth of property. The Negroes

From "Harper's Magazine" Copyright, 1864, by Harper & Brothers.

HAMPTON HOSPITAL (1862)

remaining in Hampton crossed the Creek and took refuge within the Union lines.

Fort Monroe and all the peninsula as far as Hampton bridge were at this time in the hands of the Federal troops under General Butler. The main body of the army occupied Camp Hamilton, a wilderness of tents lying between the Mill Creek bridge and the present grounds of Hampton Institute. On both sides of Mill Creek were large granaries and also cattle yards, which were filled with two or three thousand head of cattle for the Army of the Potomac. The main building of the Soldiers' Home was used as an officers' hospital and was known as Chesapeake Hospital. This was connected by a bridge with the Hampton Hospital, the general receiving point for sick and wounded soldiers of the armies in Virginia. It was organized in August 1862,* and between that time and April 1864, 6,540 patients were received. The hospital was placed on the present site of Hampton Institute and was a picturesque village of about thirty cottage houses, one hundred and twenty-five by twenty-five feet, forming a triangle which embraced a large lawn. A farm of a hundred acres was attached to the hospital and was cultivated mainly by "contrabands," who flocked by thousands to the peninsula seeking the protection of the Federal army. Twelve hundred of them were landed in one night at Old Point wharf. The

---

* For many of the facts relating to the Hampton Hospital we are indebted to an article which appeared in *Harper's Magazine* for August 1864.

road passing the hospital ran in a nearly straight line from the Hampton bridge to the officers' hospital and was provided with a horse-car line for the transportation of men and supplies. In 1864 the convalescent soldiers built Bethesda Chapel in what was afterwards the Soldiers' Cemetery, and this was for a time the only church in Hampton in which services were held. The town was occupied during the war chiefly by contrabands, who built rude shelters against the chimneys that survived the fire, and for some years afterward only small, one-story frame buildings were to be found there. The twentieth-century visitor to the trim little city, with its brick blocks, paved streets, electric railways, and handsome dwellings, finds it difficult to picture the war-time desolation.

X
HAMPTON SCHOOLS BETWEEN 1850 AND 1870

ELIZABETH City County has the honor not only of being the home of the first free school in America but of being one of the only two counties in the state which voted for a free-school system nearly twenty years before its establishment throughout the South in 1870. In the old records of this county is the following entry: "At a county court held January 25th, 1851, it was resolved that the present Board of School Commissioners for this county be appointed a committee to meet at their earliest convenience and lay off this county in School Districts as directed by the new Code of Virginia and report to the Court." On referring to the "new Code" we find that this order to divide the county into school districts must have followed the adoption, by a vote of the county, of the public-school system authorized by an Act of the Assembly of 1845-46; it indicates that there was, even at that early day, a strong public sentiment in Hampton in favor of education at public expense. Previous to this time the children of the county had been educated at the Syms-Eaton

Hampton Schools

Academy,* a consolidation of the two free schools established in the seventeenth century by Benjamin Syms (1634) and Thomas Eaton (1659). The funds owned by the trustees of this institution were not sufficient for its entire support, and many children were permitted to attend who paid tuition, thus supplementing the fund. The instruction they received was of a high grade and the principalship was considered an honor. Mr. John B. Cary was its last principal, serving for seven years, until it became a part of the free-school system in 1851. By an act of the Assembly the new Board of School Commissioners became the successors of the "Board of Trustees and Governors" of the Syms-Eaton Academy and were invested with all the property belonging to that board. This amounted to about ten thousand dollars, the interest of which was used to supplement the local tax levy for school purposes. Other schools were established in the various districts, and the subjects taught were changed to those of the ordinary district school. From Mrs. Armstrong's pamphlet on the Syms-Eaton Academy we learned that "the mortgage bonds in which the Syms-Eaton fund had been invested were in the hands of Colonel J. C. Phillips (of Hampton), and were taken by his family with their own papers when, early in

---

* For a full account of the Syms-Eaton Academy see a pamphlet on the subject by the late Mrs. Wm. Armstrong, for sale by the Hampton Chapter of the Association for the Preservation of Virginia Antiquities. Address Miss Dorothy Armstrong, Hampton, Va.

CHESAPEAKE FEMALE COLLEGE

Hampton Schools

the war, they refugeed to Richmond. Thanks to a faithful guardianship the little bundle of deeds passed safely through the risks of fire and flight and siege, and were at the end brought back to be once more recorded as 'Those bonds which are payable to the Trustees of Hampton Academy, and now, by operation of the Statutes, the property of the County School Board of Elizabeth City County.'" The interest of this fund is still used to help defray the expenses of the public schools of the county.

In 1851 Mr. Cary established an excellent school called the Hampton Military Academy, which was attended by young men and women from all parts of Virginia and other Southern states, many of whom afterwards became distinguished. Among them were Captain James Barron Hope of Norfolk, Captain Gordon McCabe of Richmond, and Colonel Thomas Tabb of Hampton; the last was both pupil and teacher there. Both ancient and modern languages were taught, as well as music and mathematics. The discipline was strict, "Order is Heaven's first law" being the motto of the school. The educational and moral ideas were of the highest and the equipment among the best of the time. Mr. Cary's old pupils speak of him with enthusiasm. He was like Arnold of Rugby—a great teacher. At the breaking out of war Mr. Cary was commissioned by General Lee major of all the Hampton troops, and was afterwards promoted for gallantry at Bethel to be lieutenant colonel of the thirty-second Virginia regiment commanded by

Hampton Schools

Colonel Ewell, President of William and Mary College. After the war, Colonel Cary returned to Richmond where he served as superintendent of public schools and in various capacities on school boards, always showing marked ability as an educator.

In 1854 there was established near Hampton another school which was well known during its short existence, the Chesapeake Female College —now the main building of the National Soldiers' Home. It was built by a Baptist minister, one Martin Forey, who however failed to make a success of it and sold it in 1859 to a board of trustees. A Colonel Raymond was principal until the war broke out and the school was disbanded. It was used during the war as a hospital for wounded officers and was afterwards purchased by General Butler who sold it to the Government.

When Hampton was burned in 1861 nothing was left of the old schools or in fact of the town. The walls of St. John's Church were left standing and those of one or two houses. Many chimneys survived the fire and against these were built temporary shacks. When the hospital wards were sold many of them were utilized in the town—some of them for stores and several for the hotel, which also made use of hospital beds, tables, and chairs. While the old church was being rebuilt through the faithful efforts of the few remaining members of the society, the handful of worshipers had service, more or less irregularly, in the Odd Fellows' Hall on Court Street, known as Patrick Henry

The Butler School for Contrabands

Hampton Schools

Hall. The first regular rector after the war was the Rev. J. B. McCarty, who had been a chaplain in the Federal army and who gave his services to St. John's Parish for two years, winning the love and confidence of all with whom he came in contact.

During the war there were no youth in Hampton to go to school except the thousands of Negro contrabands who flocked to the peninsula. Here were children of all ages eager to learn to read. Who was to teach them? The lower peninsula was occupied by the Federal army. It became the duty of the North to provide schools for the freedmen, at least temporarily. As early as 1861 there were six hundred fugitives in the vicinity of Fort Monroe. The first teacher to come from the North was the Rev. J. C. Lockwood, sent by the American Missionary Association, who opened a school on September 17, 1861, in the Red Cottage near the Chesapeake Female College, which was taught by Mrs. Peake, an educated colored woman. By the end of October Mr. Lockwood had started four other schools all taught by colored teachers. In 1862 Captain Charles B. Wilder was appointed superintendent of contrabands, and soon afterwards the courthouse in Hampton, whose walls had survived the fire, was fitted up for a graded school. The number of refugees and the number of schools continued to increase until in December 1864 there were in Hampton and its vicinity five schools with about seven hundred pupils. In 1865 the courthouse reverted to the county authorities and the

Hampton Schools

graded school for freedmen was transferred to the Lincoln School, which had been built of old hospital wards. In this year also, the large school for the contrabands built by General Butler in 1863 was made over to the American Missionary Association by General Howard. A year later there were fourteen hundred pupils in the day schools and three hundred in the night schools.

The question of the advisability of establishing a training school for colored teachers in this vicinity now began to be discussed in the *American Missionary Magazine*. In March 1866, Captain Wilder had been succeeded by General Samuel C. Armstrong as superintendent of contrabands and officer in charge of the Freedmen's Bureau. From the beginning he took special interest in the schools, having charge of those in ten counties in eastern Virginia. It was his suggestion that Hampton would be a fitting spot for a permanent training school for colored teachers. In a letter written in July 1867 he offered his services to the American Missionary Association, and when it was finally decided by that organization to establish a normal school at Hampton, General Armstrong, with his missionary inheritance, his war experience with colored troops, and his common-sense ideas of the development of character by self-help, was felt to be the proper person to put at its head. The Chesapeake Hospital was suggested for the site of the school but by General Armstrong's earnest advice this was rejected and "Little Scotland," or the Wood plantation, consisting of one hundred and

THE BEGINNINGS OF HAMPTON INSTITUTE

Hampton Schools

twenty-five acres, was purchased. The school was opened in April 1868 with two teachers and fifteen pupils, its main building consisting of remodelled hospital wards, the other buildings being the old mansion house of the plantation and Wood's mill transformed into a dwelling house. Such was the humble beginning of an institution now known throughout the civilized world as the pioneer of industrial schools, and which has more than twelve hundred students, and over six thousand graduates and ex-students. In 1870 The Hampton Normal and Agricultural Institute ceased to be a school of the American Missionary Association, being incorporated as a private institution under a special Act of the Virginia Legislature. In the same year a system of public schools for both races was established in Virginia.

XI

VIRGINIA'S SECOND COLONIAL CAPITAL, WILLIAMSBURG

THE capital of the Virginia Colony was transferred in 1698 from Jamestown to Williamsburg, seven miles away in a "more salubrious situation." The visitor to the "Cradle of the Republic" who would follow the fortunes of the little colony, drives across the causeway connecting the island with the mainland, and along the same winding, sandy road over which the early settlers traveled in the last years of the seventeenth century, leaving behind them their homes and their church in the little village on the river bank where they had seen much misery, but also, mayhap, much happiness. Williamsburg, or "Middle Plantation," was at this time but thirty-six years old and life there was most primitive. Stools and benches and strong four-posters constituted the furniture of the rude pioneer cabins and the horse trough served as the family wash-basin. But after it became the capital conditions improved rapidly, substantial houses appeared, and silver as well as pewter began to shine on polished mahogany sideboards.

Even before this the colonists, most of whom were not in sympathy with Governor Berkeley

Virginia's Second Colonial Capital

when he thanked God there were no free schools in Virginia and hoped there would be none for a hundred years, had begun to plan seriously for some opportunity for higher education if only that they need not be at the expense of sending their sons to England when they wished to study for a profession. To be sure, Harvard College had been founded, but to go from Virginia to Massachusetts in those days was almost as much of an undertaking as to go to England. So in 1691 Commissary Blair (the same whose body now lies in the ancient graveyard at Jamestown) went across the water seeking a charter for a college. He succeeded in obtaining an appropriation of two thousand pounds in money and twenty thousand acres of land, with a tax of "a penny a pound on all tobacco exported from Maryland and Virginia, together with the fees and profits arising from the office of surveyor-general." The Commissary returned triumphant, with his charter and his contributions and was forthwith made President of William and Mary College, which office he held for fifty years. The college was for some time as English as its name, the teachers being appointed by the Bishop of London who retained for himself the office of Chancellor. It was not alone for the education of their children that the Virginia colonists were solicitous. They felt a responsibility for the Indians among whom they were living and very early in the history of William and Mary the income from the English landed estate of Brafferton was set aside for the use of the Indians, a special building by

Virginia's Second Colonial Capital

that name being put up for them. The first Commencement of the college was held in 1700 and excited much interest, the roads being filled with coaches and the river with sloops from the outlying plantations and even from New York, Pennsylvania, and Maryland, while the Indians in gala costume came in afoot and added to the picturesqueness of the scene.

The college was designed by Sir Christopher Wren, and was a substantial brick building of two stories with dormer windows in the roof; it contained, besides dormitories and classrooms, a library, and a chapel extending to the rear. Here the House of Burgesses met until 1705 when the capitol was built at the opposite end of the straight, mile-long Duke of Gloucester Street. This was also a plain, two-story brick building but in the form of the letter H, with a portico in front. Hard by was the Raleigh Tavern, a wooden building, one full story in height with an attic above lit by eight dormer windows in each wing. There was an entrance door near the centre of each front and over one of these a leaden bust of Sir Walter Raleigh. Its most famous apartment was the Apollo Room, which had a deep fireplace with a door on either side and was adorned with a carved wainscoting under the windows and over the mantel. When Spottswood became governor in 1714, the Governor's Palace, midway between the college and the capitol on an estate of four hundred acres, was added to this group of historic buildings. In a public square in the centre of the

WILLIAM AND MARY COLLEGE

Virginia's Second Colonial Capital

town, Spottswood built also, in obedience to an Act of the Burgesses, the octagonal brick Powder Horn with its quaint, steep-pitched roof. When first built it was surrounded by an outer wall and formed a complete magazine, with powder room, armory, and blacksmith shop.

About this same time, in 1715, Bruton Church was completed, being built on plans made by the same energetic and versatile Governor Spottswood. This church was the centre of the interesting group of buildings in Old Williamsburg. Cruciform in shape, the long arm abutted on the Palace Green and stretched along the Duke of Gloucester Street, having a tower at the western end towards the college. It was built, like all the other early public buildings, of brick made in English moulds, and over these, especially at the eastern end, the ivy soon threw a mantle of green. The windows were made of small square panes of plain white glass and most of them are still unbroken in spite of the ravages of two wars. The churchyard was enclosed by a low brick wall with a stone coping, the land being the gift of Sir John Page, ancestor of the present Page family of Rosewell in Gloucester County. Flagstone walks led to the church doors and the aisles within were paved with the same material. Up these aisles from the tower entrance walked the stately Burgesses when they met for prayer before proceeding to the business of state, and here walked also each Sunday and on fast days the court processions—the governor and the council of state in their gorgeous robes and

Virginia's Second Colonial Capital

carrying emblazoned banners. The governor's pew, elevated, large, and square, and canopied with rich crimson velvet, occupied one of the corners made by the meeting of the transepts and nave, and the high pulpit with its sounding board was placed on the opposite corner, the choir behind it as in English cathedrals, and the chancel at the eastern end.

It was a gay little capital—Old Williamsburg—so gay that it was said to resemble the Court of St. James. Withal it was picturesque. Gentlemen rode dressed in bright colored velvets and ruffles, the clergy in dignified black, and the judges in scarlet, while the mechanics appeared in red flannel shirts, and with leathern aprons over buckskin breeches. The students of William and Mary wore academic dress. It was the age of the hoopskirt, and on dress occasions such as a ball at Governor Spottswood's, the ladies wore over the hoopskirt trailing gowns of heavy brocade, while their hair was dressed very high and adorned with feathers, ribbons, and lace. The Colonial governors lived in great state, driving to public functions in a carriage drawn by six milk-white horses. Their families and those of the House of Burgesses added much to the brilliancy of the social life. In the middle of the eighteenth century theatre going was added to the list of Colonial entertainments, the "Charming Sally" bringing from England a company of players in charge of Lewis Hallam, who presented "The Merchant of Venice" to Williamsburg society.

But life there was not a mere butterfly existence.

BRUTON PARISH CHURCH

Virginia's Second Colonial Capital

In attendance at William and Mary were the makers of the nation—for the nation was then in maning—Jefferson, the author of the Declaration of Independence; Harrison, Braxton, Nelson, and Wythe, four of its signers; Peyton Randolph, President of the First Continental Congress; and many others prominent in Revolutionary history. Washington took his degree as civil engineer at this college and was its first American Chancellor. It was in Williamsburg in her mansion on the Six Chimney Lot that he wooed and won the Widow Custis. At the capitol Patrick Henry was a prominent figure and his emphatic words, "If that be treason, make the most of it," resounded from its walls. With Washington and Jefferson in legislative assembly in 1769, he drew up the famous resolutions asserting that the people of Virginia could be taxed only by their own representatives, and declaring it to be both lawful and expedient for all the colonies to unite in protest against any violation of American rights. Henry was one of those who, when the assembly was dissolved by Lord Botetourt and again when it was disbanded by Lord Dunmore, retired to the Apollo Room of the Raleigh Tavern, the last time passing those resolutions which resulted in the assembling of the First Continental Congress. The Apollo Room of the Raleigh probably witnessed "more scenes of brilliant festivity and political excitement than any other single apartment in North America."

Little Williamsburg was the birthplace of the Revolution. In other parts of the Colony the fires

Virginia's Second Colonial Capital

of revolution smouldered until fanned into flame by Dunmore's stealing of the powder and his wanton act in the burning of Norfolk. Then indeed the demand for liberty became imperative and a resolution was unanimously passed instructing the Virginia delegates to ask Congress to declare the United Colonies free and independent states. When the news was received in Williamsburg the town went wild, church bells were rung, guns fired, and the British flag was hauled down from the capitol, the thirteen stripes being run up in its stead.

After this demonstration things seem to have quieted down at the little capital; the scene had shifted to the Northern battlefields. It was in December of the first year of the war that the Phi Beta Kappa Society, the oldest Greek letter fraternity in the United States, was organized at William and Mary, and it was in 1779 that the college was reorganized by Jefferson and the elective system introduced. High tide had been reached in its affairs. During the Revolution it lost its most important sources of revenue and has never regained its former prestige. Virginia did not become the battlefield until Cornwallis began his retreat down the peninsula in June 1781. Lafayette followed him closely and on July 6 an action took place at Green Spring, once Governor Berkeley's country home, where the Americans were repulsed. Cornwallis then occupied Yorktown and the surrender followed in October. At this time Bruton Church was used as a hospital. During its occupancy by Lafayette's troops, the house of the president of William and

Virginia's Second Colonial Capital

Mary, a fine specimen of eighteenth century architecture, was accidentally destroyed by fire, but was restored by King Louis XVI from his private funds. This house was used at one time as the headquarters of Cornwallis. Washington later had his headquarters in the home of Chancellor Wythe on Palace Green.

After the Revolution and the transference of the capital to Richmond, Williamsburg lost its importance, and the present visitor to the little city finds it a dreamy, charming, restful spot, quiet and aristocratic, its Court and Palace Greens dotted with buttercups among which cattle browse, the old churchyard overgrown, and the stones crumbling away. The site of the "magnificent" Palace with its cupola illuminated on the King's birth-night, is occupied by a free school of the American Republic, and its "grounds" have disappeared. In place of the famous Raleigh Tavern has risen a modern dry-goods store, and though the Duke of Gloucester Street still stretches from the college to the site of the capitol, whose foundations have been marked out by the Colonial Chapter of the A. P. V. A., it is grass grown and is no longer filled with gorgeous equipages or with gaily caparisoned horses. Chancellor Wythe's house remains, haunted by many ghosts, also the homes of Peyton and Edmund Randolph, and of Wm. Wirt, John Marshall, and John Blair, with their quaint stone steps, Colonial doorways, and brass knockers, with their dormer windows, "offices," and old rose gardens. Williamsburg has charming interiors—large rooms furnished with

Virginia's Second Colonial Capital

antique furniture, paintings of ancestors by famous artists of the last century, delightful old brasses, curious bits of china, and here and there a glimpse of a Chippendale staircase or chair. The old Garrett home there was spoken of in a *Virginia Gazette* of 1763. The oldest part of the house has a quaint staircase; the only one like it in Virginia is at Lower Brandon on the James. The front porch is tiled with square red brick tiles like those in one of the old chancels at Jamestown, and its door has a curious old knocker of colored brass, showing its antiquity.

In the center of the town still stand two buildings designed by Sir Christopher Wren, the courthouse, built in 1769, and the old Powder Horn, which has seen many vicissitudes, having been alternately a market, a school, a church, and a dancing school. It is now a museum and contains memorial windows to Nathaniel Bacon, Jr., "the rebel," and Alexander Spottswood, "the best governor Virginia ever had."

Bruton Church was "remodeled" in 1840 so as to be fairly unrecognizable with its partition midway of the nave and its chancel against the partition. The town clock which was put into the steeple at that time ceased for many years to mark the flight of time but has now been put in order and strikes the hours. The Jamestown font from which Pocahontas is said to have been baptized is one of the valued possessions of Bruton Church, which has also fallen heir to the Jamestown communion service bearing the date 1661, and owns two others

The Courthouse at Williamsburg

Virginia's Second Colonial Capital

which are highly prized—the Queen Anne set, of silver gilt, beautifully chased, and the King George service of solid silver bearing the royal insignia. Underneath the church and in the old graveyard lie buried many men and women whose names are known to history, and one may wander for hours there deciphering the old inscriptions and living in the past. The old church was again used as a hospital during the Civil War after the battle of Fort Magruder. It has recently been restored in accordance with its original design, the governor's pew having its canopy of rich crimson velvet which bears upon it the royal arms of England, sent from that country as the gift of the Spottswood family. President Roosevelt has presented the church with a lectern, on which will rest a Bible, the gift of King Edward of England, to be presented by the Bishop of London at the time of the meeting of the General Convention in October 1907.

William and Mary College is not only, alive but prospering. Its main building was burned in 1862 after ninety per cent of the students had left to go to the Civil War. But it was rebuilt on the old plan and looks much as it did when first designed. Brafferton Hall was not long an Indian school but is still used as one of the college buildings. In 1888 a normal department was added which now attracts the larger number of students. The statue of Lord Botetourt, much defaced, stands in the walk halfway between the gate and the college. His body rests beneath the college chapel with those of General Nelson and Peyton Randolph. Several new

Virginia's Second Colonial Capital

buildings indicate the present prosperity of the college. In the interesting and ancient library which has a valuable Virginia department, and whose walls are lined with engravings, portraits, and maps, the the charter of the Phi Beta Kappa, and many other relics, are preserved files of the *Virginia Gazette,* the *Southern Literary Messenger,* and many valuable antiques, among them the first edition of Thomson's Seasons printed in London in 1730, and a copy of Livy printed in Venice in 1498.

XII

YORKTOWN—THE WATERLOO OF THE REVOLUTION

AMONG the Indians living in Eastern Virginia under the dominion of King Powhatan were the Cheskiacks, who had a village on a bluff overlooking the York (then called the Pamunkey) and distant only ten or twelve miles from his capital—Werawocomoco. This was the first settlement on the site of Yorktown. Later these Indians moved across the river into Gloucester County, and colonists settled in 1630 on or near the site of their village, keeping its Indian name but changing the name of the river to the Charles. To keep out the savages and give the settlers a chance to raise cattle, it was proposed to build a palisade stretching from "Cheskiack on the Charles to Martin's Hundred (where Carter's Grove now stands) on the Powhatan," and this was actually done in 1634 at a cost of twelve hundred pounds. Although it took one hundred pounds a year to keep this palisade in repair, it probably more than paid for itself in the profit that accrued to the colonists from the stock they were able to raise within it. A court was held on Charles River in this same year, probably on the spot now known as Temple Farm, from the ruins of a church with double walls found there,

The Waterloo of the Revolution

which are believed by the antiquarian, President Tyler of William and Mary College, to be those of the village church of York Parish. This plantation was afterwards the summer home of Governor Spottswood and is now known as the Moore House.

At Cheskiack was built one of the five warehouses in the Colony, to which planters were obliged to bring their crops to be inspected and from which they could be taken only to be shipped to England. Later, in order to increase the importance of Jamestown, the capital, they were required to send their tobacco there to be shipped. Doubtless there was much evasion of these laws and the cave now known as Cornwallis's Cave was probably dug out of the bluff by some enterprising planter to assist in this evasion.

The "city" of Yorktown had its birth in the Act for Ports passed in 1691 which required the owners of certain plantations to sell town sites of fifty acres each for ten thousand pounds of tobacco. In York County it was the plantation of Benjamin Read from which fifty acres were sold and laid off in half-acre lots to establish Yorktown on what was henceforth known as the York River. And so, having a school and church, custom house and courthouse, stocks and pillory, the "city" led a placid eixstence for nearly a century, cultivating the same fields that the Indians had, though impoverishing the once fertile soil by continual planting of tobacco. The planters shipped their money crop (tobacco) to England and received in exchange the necessities of life; for recreation they fished and sailed on their broad river,

The Main Street of Yorktown

The Waterloo of the Revolution

enjoying all the gayeties of pre-Revolutionary life in the Virginia Colony.

That life in Yorktown was not too primitive may be judged from the appearance of the Nelson House, a fine specimen of Colonial architecture with its lofty rooms and solid walls. Up and down its circular stone steps fashionable Colonial dames tripped to party or ball or to a visit at a neighboring plantation, and numerous gallants no doubt attended them. The small windows, solid shutters, and massive door indicate that even in the midst of the gayety there was need of protection from attack by the Indians. George Mason, Washington, Jefferson, and Lafayette have slept in this house and thither Cornwallis retired after being shelled out of Secretary Nelson's house on the hill. The historic mansion of the Nelsons was built by Thomas Nelson, known as "Scotch Tom," the father of William Nelson, President of the King's Council, and the grandfather of General Thomas Nelson, signer of the Declaration of Independence and war Governor of Virginia, the most patriotic and illustrious of his race. When money was needed to pay the troops during the Revolution and to run the Government, as Virginia's credit was low, he borrowed money on his personal credit to such an extent that after his death his vast estates went for the public debts, leaving his family penniless.

Quiet little Yorktown suddenly became, in 1781, the central figure of the Revolutionary stage. In order to capture Arnold, who had burned Richmond and raided the plantations on the James River,

The Waterloo of the Revolution

Washington decided to send both the American and French forces into Virginia. Cornwallis, assuming command of the British forces, sent Arnold back to New York and tried to destroy Lafayette's army in the interior of Virginia, but not succeeding in this he returned to the sea and was ordered to entrench himself at Yorktown. How securely he did this and how when he wished to leave his trenches he could not, being completely hemmed in and at the mercy of the combined forces under the personal command of Washington, all the world knows.

If you visit Yorktown to-day, what you may not remember of the eleven-day siege will be recalled to your memory by the intensely patriotic and enthusiastic keeper of the National Cemetery hard by the battlefield. He will show you in the distance the line of breastworks completely encircling the village, with Fort Hamilton on the right overgrown with clambering blackberry vines, and the whole circle gay with the yellow flowers of the broom; and though you know that these are fortifications of a later struggle and that the redoubt taken by dashing young Colonel Hamilton has long since disappeared, you do not refuse to give your imagination rein and repeople the trenches before Yorktown. You see Washington's line forming a crescent before the breastworks; on the right American troops under Lafayette, on the left the French under Rochambeau. You see De Grasse's fleet in the river, the tall masts rising over the bluff, and you realize that no retreat for the British is possible that way. You

The Waterloo of the Revolution

trace out the lines of the first parallel and see Washington putting the match to the first gun with his own hand. You hear the cannonade begin and continue almost without interruption for four days. What a target that house on the hill is! It is Secretary Nelson's, and Cornwallis is there. The venerable secretary is permitted to join his sons within the American lines and then shell after shell strikes the house until Cornwallis must needs find better protection behind the solid shutters and stone walls of the old Nelson mansion. The master of that mansion is leading in person the State militia, and, seeing his troops' hesitation to injure the old house, himself trains a gun on the enemy's retreat.

You see the second parallel established and hear the resolve to storm the place. You join gallant young Hamilton in his sortie and are close behind him when he mounts the works from the shoulder of one of his men and shouts, "Tell the Baron (the French officer who was attacking the other redoubt) that my redoubt is carried and ask where he is." "Tell the Marquis," answered the Frenchman, "that I am not in mine but will be in five minutes." You see that the whole British line of works is captured and that the contest is practically decided. You are thinking of the desperate efforts made by the British to escape—of the attempts to retake the works, to run the gauntlet of the fleet, to get across to Gloucester Point and join Tarleton—when you are suddenly brought back to the present by the voice of the old keeper: "Yes, sir, God Almighty won that battle, sir. Yes, sir, didn't He send a big

The Waterloo of the Revolution

storm and a black night and make the British turn back? Yes, sir, He did. The Lord be praised." And now he tells you that you are standing just where the British army marched slowly and dejectedly out, carrying their arms and with colors cased, between the American and French ranged in lines a mile long on either side of the road. Washington was on horseback with his aides at the head of the American line and Count Rochambeau, similarly surrounded, at the head of the French line. Cornwallis, who had signed the articles of capitulation in the Moore House three hours before, was represented by one of his generals who conducted the surrender. A monument, recently erected, marks the probable site of the event.

You drive on by a broom-bordered and grass-grown road to the Moore House on a bluff near the shore about a mile from the village, and look with interest at the spot where one of the most momentous events in the history of America took place. The antique roof and the rooms with corner fireplaces bespeak the age of the house, and its situation on the breezy bluff indicates the attraction it had for busy Governor Spottswood when he wished to rest from the cares of state in the gay little capital, Williamsburg. Driving into sleepy old Yorktown, which has evidently never recovered from the bombardment, you stop to examine the tall and stately monument erected to the American soldiers who fell during the siege, and note in the village the ancient custom house, once the fashionable rendezvous for the young gentlemen about town. That it

THE MOORE HOUSE, YORKTOWN

The Waterloo of the Revolution

is the oldest one in America is very easy to believe as you examine its moss-covered, peaked roof, thick walls, and massive oaken doors and shutters. The Nelson House still remains to tell of past prosperity, and a little old church stands on the hill with the graves beside it of the illustrious men who helped to make their country free—three generations of Nelsons—and beside them their friends and neighbors.

But a short distance up the York River, on the Gloucester side, stands the Page homestead, Rosewell, a fine old Colonial mansion; and on land belonging to the estate, near Werowocomoco, is an interesting relic called Powhatan's Chimney, said to have belonged to a house built for Powhatan by John Smith in response to the Indian monarch's requisition for "a house, a grindstone, fifty swords, some guns, a cock and hen, with much copper, and many beads." The fireplace is wide enough to roast an ox. It was at Werowocomoco that Pocahontas saved the life of John Smith.

XIII

RICHMOND AND THE JAMES RIVER PLANTATIONS

ON June 29, 1776, the Virginia Colony ceased to be and the Commonwealth began. The Convention of 1775, on account of Lord Dunmore's attitude, had been obliged to leave the Colonial capital—Williamsburg—and met in St. John's Church in the little village of Richmond. Here Patrick Henry, soon to be made Governor of the Commonwealth, made his world-famous speech, ending with the oft-quoted words: "Give me liberty or give me death." The public records soon followed the Convention, for safekeeping, and with them the offices of the government; thus Richmond became Virginia's third capital, by the necessities of war, the removal being made legal in 1779 by an Act of the Assembly.

At this time there were less than three hundred houses in Richmond, for it had not been in existence much more than thirty years, and towns in those days did not grow, like mushrooms, in a single night. It was founded by Colonel William Byrd of Westover on the James, who wrote in 1733 in his "Journey to the Land of Eden": "When we got home we laid the foundations of two large cities—one at Shacco's to be called Richmond and the other

The Old Capitol, Richmond

Photograph by Cook

The James River Plantations

at the Point of Appamattucks River to be named Petersburg." The invitation to all people to come to Richmond to live was published in the first Colonial newspaper, the *Virginia Gazette*, established in 1736. It was settled almost wholly by Scotch or Irish merchants and nothing of importance, save skirmishes with the Indians, happened there until the traitor Arnold moved against it when he invaded Virginia in 1781. Anchoring near Jamestown he went the next day as far as Westover, below Richmond which then had a popluation of only eighteen hundred persons, half of whom were slaves. Arnold landed his troops and marched into the town, meeting with no resistance, for Jefferson, then Governor, unable to assemble an adequate force of militia, had taken the public records and gone with them to a place of safety. The cannon factory on the hill was destroyed, many buildings were burned, and all the tobacco in the place went up in smoke. All this Arnold did in twenty-four hours and then retired to Westover, giving Jefferson a chance to come back!

After the close of the Revolutionary War Richmond began to grow into a city. The capitol, finished in 1789, was built after a model brought by Jefferson from France, which may still be seen in the State Library. It is a stucco copy of the Maison Carrée in Nismes, France, a Roman temple built by Augustus Caesar as a memorial to his two sons who had been killed in battle. Probably no building in the United States has been the scene of more famous debates and certainly no legislative halls have heard the voices of more distinguished statesmen. The roll call is a long one—Tyler, Mason, Madison, Monroe, Jefferson, Wythe, Chief Justice Marshall, John Randolph of Roanoke. In 1861 the accidents of war again made Richmond a capital, this time of the Confederate States, and the Confederate Congress during the four years of its existence met in the capitol building. Recently two large wings have been added to it, making it much more beautiful and imposing. In the rotunda stands Houdon's famous statue of Washington, said to be one of the most priceless pieces of marble in the world. The equestrian statue of Washington in Capitol Square is also a wonderful piece of work. It was drawn by hand by enthusiastic citizens from the ship landing to its present position. Around the pedestal of the monument stand figures of some of the "founders of the nation"—Virginians all—George Mason, Thomas Jefferson, Andrew Lewis, Patrick Henry, James Madison, and John Marshall. Richmond is a city of monuments. Prominent among the others are the equestrian statue of Lee and the monument to Stonewall Jackson.

Richmond churches are closely associated with its history—St. John's, the oldest, with Patrick Henry and the Convention of 1788, made up of such men as Madison, Monroe, Marshall, Mason, Wythe, Pendleton, Harrison, and Edmund Randolph. The Monumental Church is built upon the site of the theatre which was burned in 1811 with great loss of life, and contains in an urn the ashes of the victims, among whom was the governor of the state.

HISTORIC ST. JOHN'S, RICHMOND

Photograph by Cook

The James River Plantations

Bishop Moore and Bishop Meade have both preached in this church. St. Paul's has the distinction of having given its bell to be cast into cannon for use in the Civil War. President Davis and General Lee worshiped there, and there Mr. Davis received the telegram announcing that the lines had been broken at Petersburg and that Richmond would have to be evacuated. The home of the President, known as the "White House of the Confederacy," is now the Confederate Museum. General Lee's family lived during the war in what is at present the home of the Virginia Historical Society.

The capital of the Confederacy was of course the strategic point of the struggle of 1861-5. No less than fifteen pitched battles and twenty-five skirmishes were fought in its vicinity during those years, and the Confederate army was besieged in the city for nearly a year before it was evacuated. Libby Prison, whose name and history are so well known, is no longer in Richmond, having been removed to Chicago at the time of the World's Fair. These few sentences suggest pages of both written and unwritten history. In beautiful Hollywood Cemetery overlooking the James rest twelve thousand Southern soldiers and the President who represented their cause. Here, too, lie the bodies of the United States Presidents Monroe and Tyler, of Henry A. Wise, war Governor of Virginia, Bishop Meade, and John Randolph of Roanoke.

In the last forty years Richmond has increased rapidly in population and prosperity until it is now the largest and wealthiest city in the state. As in

The James River Plantations

Colonial years it is closely associated with the plantations on the James, for their owners in many cases have houses in the capital also. The Byrds of Westover, the Harrisons of Berkeley and Brandon, and the Carters of Shirley are names as well known in Richmond as in their stately mansions overlooking the broad "Powhatan." The founder of Virginia's capital, Honorable William Evelyn Byrd, sleeps in the garden at Westover under a monument on which the curious may read his biography. He was the most illustrious of his line—"one of the brightest stars in the social skies of Colonial Virginia." He was the author of the Westover MSS., a fascinating account of plantation life in his generation. His "Memoirs," published several years ago, are also of great interest. His daughter, "The Fair Evelyn," whose portrait hangs in the drawing room at Lower Brandon, was the greatest beauty of her time and has been appropriated by Mary Johnston as one of the characters in "Audrey." Westover house is one of the best specimens of Colonial architecture in America. All the lofty rooms are wainscoted to the ceiling; the twisted balustrades of the stairs at the back of the great hall are of solid mahogany. The vandalism of the soldiers during the Civil War destroyed much of quaint interest and priceless value, but the restoration has been thorough and the house is probably the best preserved of Virginia Colonial houses.

Berkeley, the adjoining plantation, was the birthplace of President Harrison. It also is in a good state of preservation. In common with most of the

Lower Brandon

The James River Plantations

other James River plantations, it suffered severely in the Indian massacre of 1622. Shirley, the seat of the Carters, was laid out in 1611 by Sir Thomas Dale, Governor of the Colony, who took an active part in forwarding the marriage of Rolfe and Pocahontas. Shirley was so "well fortified" during the Indian massacre in 1622 that it was a place of refuge and no one was killed there. Soon after their marriage Rolfe and Pocahontas moved to Varina, which was probably the birthplace of their son, Thomas Rolfe, from whom many Virginians are proud to own their descent. All the James River families and indeed all old Virginia families are related to one another, as the names plainly show—Carter Page, Carter Harrison, Byrd Harrison, etc. At Brandon, just above Jamestown, lived another branch of the Harrison family. The wings of the Lower Brandon house were built by Nathaniel Harrison about 1712. His son, Benjamin Harrison, was a roommate of Thomas Jefferson's at William and Mary and the latter planned the square central part of the Lower Brandon house. This plantation was pillaged by Arnold during the Revolution and raided by General Butler's troops in the Civil War, when the outbuildings were burned and the stock stolen; the mansion was seriously injured and would have been destroyed but for a telegram from President Lincoln forbidding it. Fortunately the ladies of the household had left for Richmond two days before, carrying with them everything of value that was movable. The house is still owned by Harrisons and shows signs of the ravages of war in the dents

The James River Plantations

made by bullets over the door and in other ways within the house. It contains valuable old silver, and historic portraits. Upper Brandon was originally included in the Brandon estate. The house was severely damaged during the war and has never been fully restored. Carter's Grove, below Jamestown, is a fine old mansion built by "King" Carter, a wealthy Colonial planter. It was the scene in Jefferson's time of his unsuccessful wooing of Rebecca Burwell.

INDEX

Archer's Hope, 12
Armstrong, Gen. S. C., 78-79
Arnold, Benedict, 93, 99, 103
Artillery School, 26
A. P. V. A., work of preservation at Jamestown, 11, 14, 15; Williamsburg, 87
Bacon's Castle, 12
Bacon's Rebellion, 10, 14, 15, 42; memorial window, 88.
Barron, Commodore James, model of iron-clad, 20; biography 62-66
Barron, Richard, 62
Barron: Samuel and James, the younger, 63
Basse's Choice, 12
Berkeley, 102
Berkeley, Sir Wm., 14, 81
Bethesda Chapel, 72
Blackbeard, 47-50; ballad, 50
Blackbeard's Point, 49, 68
Blair, Dr. James, grave, 13; commissary, 43; charter for William and Mary College, 81
Blair, Sarah, grave, 13
Bonnet, Stede, 47, 48
Botetourt, Lord, 85; statue, 89
Brafferton Hall, 43, 81, 89
Brandon, Lower, 102, 103-104
Brandon, Upper, 104
Bruton Church, 83, 86, 88-89
Bryce, Ambassador, 15
Buckroe, 38, 41
Burgesses, 10, 12; monument, 15; at Williamsburg, 82, 83
Butler, Gen. B. F., buys Soldiers' Home, 28, 76; in command Ft. Monroe, 71
Butler School, 78
Byrd, Col. Wm., founder of Richmond, 98; grave, 102
Camp Hamilton, 71
Cape Charles, 25, 46
Cape Henry, landing at, 7, 17; lighthouse, 17; 20, 25, 46
Carter's Grove, 104
Cary, Col. John B., 74, 75
Chamberlin Hotel, 28
Charles Town, resort of pirates, 45, 47
Chesapeake Bay, 16, 23, 26, 27, 59, 60
Chesapeake College, 28, 76
Cheskiack Indians, Treaty, 41; village, 91; palisade, 91
Cockburn, Admiral, 20; attack on Hampton, 68
Colonial Dames of America, 15
Contrabands, 71, 77, 78

Committee of Safety, 60, 62
Communion silver, St. John's, 56; Jamestown, 88; Bruton, 89
Cornwallis, Lord: in Hampton Roads, 64, 65, 67; Yorktown Campaign, 86; cave, 92; siege, 93-96
Craney Island, 19; battery, 20; burning of Merrimac, 20
Crutchfield, Col., 68
Cunningham, Lieut., escape, 63
Dale, Sir Thos., arrival at Kecoughtan, 35, 36
Davis, Pres. Jefferson, at Ft. Monroe, 26; in Richmond, 101
DeGrasse, Count, 24, 94
De la Warre, Lord, 9, 13, 53
Dunmore, Lord, 20; stealing of gunpowder, 59; bombardment of Norfolk, 60, 62, 85
Eaton School, see Syms School
Elizabeth River, 19, 21
Elizabeth City County; naming and extent, 36; vinedressers, 38; first free school, 40; population, 41; value of slaves, 42; property, 44; exposure to attack, 59; free-school system, 73
Fort Algernon, 38
—— Charles, 35
—— George, 23, 62
—— Henry, 35
—— Monroe, 19, history and defenses, 24, 26; in Civil War, 71, 77
—— Nelson, 21
—— Norfolk, 21
—— Wool, see Rip Raps
Fox Hill, 41
Freedmen's Bureau, 78
Gates, Sir Thos., captures Kecoughtan, 35
Garrett home, 88
Gosport Navy Yard, 20
Hamilton, Alexander, 94, 95
Hampton: early schools, 40; site, 43; old graveyard, 46; port of entry, 52; first church, 54; second church, 55; St. John's, 55; in Revolution, 62, 67; in war of 1812, 68, 69; burning, 70; schools (1850-70), 73-79
Hampton Academy, see Syms School
Hampton Hospital, 28, 71
Hampton Institute, 19; site, 55, 71; beginnings, 78, 79
Hampton Military Academy, 75

INDEX—Continued

Hampton River, *see* Southampton
Hampton Roads: 16-21; naval display at Exposition, 17; battle of Monitor and Merrimac, 18; surroundings, 19; defenses, 26; capture of pirate, 46; Virginia Navy, 61-65
Harrison, Nathaniel, 103
Henry, Patrick, 57, 58, 59; 85, 98, 100; banner, 59, 61
Hope, Mrs. Jane, 69
Hunt, Rev. Robert, tablet, 15
Hygeia Hotel, history, 27
Indians: as slaves, 42; plan to educate, 43, 44; school at Ft. Christanna, 53; Brafferton Hall, 81, 89. *See also* Kecoughtan, Chesklak Indians
Jamestown: 7-15; settlement, 7-11; site of landing, 13; shipload of maidens and first cargo of slaves, 10; saved from massacre, 12; fires, 10; desertion of, 11; breakwater, 11; "third ridge," 14; monuments, 15; Tercentennial, 15, 16, 17
Jamestown church: first, 9; first brick, 10; tower, 10, 13; foundations, 12; graveyard, 13, 14; restoration of brick, 15; communion silver, 88; font, 88
Jamestown Island: no town, 11; present condition, 12; monuments, 15
James River, 7; historic associations 12, 59; plantations, 93, 102-104
Jefferson, Thos., 57, 58, 85, 86, 99, 103, 104
Kecoughtan: 30-38; visits of John Smith, 33-35; forts, 35, 38; change of name, 36
Kecoughtan Indians: meetings with John Smith, 16, 33, 35; village and manner of life, 30-35; treaty with whites, 41
Kempsville, "Old Hundred" church, 21
Knights of Golden Horseshoe, 54
Lafayette, 86, 94; in Norfolk, 22
Lincoln School, 78
Lockwood, J. C., 77
Ludwell, Col. Philip, 14
Magruder, Gen., 70
Mallory, Col. Francis, 65
Martin's Hundred, 12, 91

Maynard, Lieut., capture of Blackbeard, 49
Merrimac (Virginia), history, 20
Middle Plantation, *see* Williamsburg
Mill Creek, 24, 28, 71
Moore House, 92, 96
Monitor and Merrimac, battle, 18
Monumental Church, Richmond, 100
National Soldiers' Home: 19; description, 28; as Chesapeake Hospital, 71; cemetery, 29
Naval Hospital, 21
Navigation Acts, responsible for piracy, 45
Navy Yard, history, 20
Necotowance, treaty, 41
Negroes: first cargo, 10; no separate churches, 39; number, 41, 42, 51; value, 42; treatment, 52; baptism, 56; Cap't Mark Starlin, 65; after burning of Hampton, 70; schools at Hampton, 77-79
Nelson, Gen. Thos., 93; grave, 97
Nelson House, 93
Newport, Cap't, 7, 11
Newport News, 11; settlement, 19
Nicholson, Gov., 44, 46
Norfolk: in War of 1812, 20; navy yard, 21, 27; settlement, 21; St. Paul's, 21; in Revolution, 21, 22; later history, 22; bombardment, 60
Oceana, Chapel by the Sea, 21
Old Point, *see* Point Comfort
Opechancanough, 13, 41
Pace's Pains, 12
Parson's school, 40
Page, Sir John, 83, 97
Peake, Mrs. Mary, 77
Petersburg, 99, 101
Pembroke Farm, graveyard, 46
Phi Beta Kappa, organized, 86
Phillips, Col. J. C., 74
Phoebus, Harrison, 28
Pirates, 45-50
Pirates' Road, 49
Pocahontas: place of marriage and baptism, 13; monument, 15; rescue of John Smith, 97; home, 102
Pochins, meeting with John Smith, 33; driven from Kecoughtan, 35
Point Comfort (Old Point): 19; naming, 23; forts, 23-28; in Civil War, 71

INDEX—Continued

Portsmouth, navy yard, 20; settlement, 21
Powder Horn, 83, 88
Powhatan, 33, 91
Powhatan oaks, 17, 22; chimney, 97
Princess Anne County, Colonial churches, 21; witch, 21, 52
Queen Anne, silver, 21, 89; bell, 56, 69
Raleigh, Sir Walter, 21, 82
Raleigh Tavern, 82, 85, 87
Ratcliffe, Cap't John, fortifies Point Comfort, 23
Richmond: 22, 93; made capital, 98; capitol, 99; Confederate capital, 100; churches, 100, 101; in Civil War, 101
Ringfield, 41
Rip Raps, location, 19; history, 25
Rochambeau, Count, 94-96
Sabbath, observance, 39, 40
St. John's Church, Hampton: 55-56; 69-70; steeple struck by lightning, 67; in Civil War, 76
St. John's Church, Richmond, 98, 100
St. Paul's Church, Norfolk, 21
St. Paul's Church, Richmond, 101
Servant, Richard B., 69
Sewell's Point, 16-20
Shirley, 103
Smith, Cap't John: monument, 15; lands at Cape Henry, 16, 17; visits Kecoughtan, 33-35; rescue by Pocahontas, 97
Smithfield church, 39
Southampton, Earl of, 35, 56
Southampton (Hampton) River: 35, 36; ferry, 42; in Revolution, 62; War of 1812, 68
Spottswood, Gov., 49, 53-54; memorial window, 88; Temple Farm, 92, 96

Syms-Eaton School, 40, 74, 75
Temple Farm, 91, 92
Tobacco: as money, 10, 43, 92; culture, 10, 38; storehouses, 42
Tyler, Lyon G., 55, 92
Varina, 102
Virginia: capes, 7, 9, 46, 49; navy, 20, 59-66; churches, 39; first free school, 40; population, 42; roads, 42; towns, 43; first college, 43; postal service, 44, 52, 53; pirates, 45-50; public-school system, 79
Virginia Gazette, 51, 52, 60, 90, 99
Virginia General Assembly: first meeting, 10, 12; roads, 42; public schools, 73, 74; Hampton Institute, 79; Richmond made capital, 98
Washington, George, 57, 58, 85, 94-96; monuments, 100
Whiting, Col. Thos., 63
Wilder, Cap't Chas. B., 77
William and Mary College: beginnings, 43, 81-82; famous students, 85; Phi Beta Kappa, 86; present condition, 89; library, 90
Williamsburg: made capital, 11, 80; Pirates' Road, 49; stealing of gunpowder, 59; historic buildings, 82, 83; social life, 84; birthplace of Revolution, 85; present appearance, 87
"Witchduck," 21
Werawocomoco, 91
Westover, 98, 99, 102
Wren, Sir Christopher, 82, 88
Wythe, Chancellor, home, 57, 87
Yeardley, Gov., 20, 56
Yorktown (Chesklack) 63; history, 91-96; custom house, 97

www.ingramcontent.com/pod-product-compliance
Lightning Source LLC
Chambersburg PA
CBHW050640160426
43194CB00010B/1755